Stories of Yuletide

by

ERNEST K. EMURIAN

Author of

Plays and Pageants for Many Occasions
More Plays and Pageants for Many Occasions
Living Stories of Famous Hymns
Famous Stories of Inspiring Hymns
Stories of Our National Songs
Living Stories of Favorite Songs
Forty True Stories of Famous Gospel Songs
Ten New Plays for Church and School
Stories of Christmas Carols
Stories of Civil War Songs

W. A. WILDE COMPANY NATICK, MASS.

STORIES OF YULETIDE

Library of Congress Catalog Card Number 60-15261

Printed in U.S.A.

To
Our First-born
Henry
who went with me
to
Oberndorf
in
1959

PREFACE

STORIES OF YULETIDE is a sequel to the author's STORIES OF CHRISTMAS CAROLS, to which readers are referred for the interesting stories of these carols: Angels from the Realms of Glory, As with Gladness Men of Old, Brightest and Best of the Sons of the Morning, Hark the Herald Angels Sing, It Came upon the Midnight Clear, Joy to the World, O Little Town of Bethlehem, Silent Night, The First Noel, We Three Kings of Orient Are and When Marshalled on the Nightly Plain.

This new volume contains the fascinating stories of the Christmas flower, the Poinsettia; a Christmas song, Up on the House-Top; a Christmas carol, Good King Wenceslaus; a Christmas poem, 'Twas the Night Before Christmas; and three familiar Christmas hymns: Thou Didst Leave Thy Throne, O Come, O Come Immanuel, In the Bleak Mid-Winter; and the most famous Christmas hymn of all, Silent Night, in the chapter entitled A Visit to Oberndorf (Austria) which the author and his son visited in the summer of 1959; in addition to seven original Christmas poems.

The origin of the word "Yule" is about as difficult to trace as that of any other word that has come down through many languages over the span of many centuries. "Yule" may have been the god of winter worshipped by the ancient Britons, or, in its other spellings, which vary from "jol" to "eule" or "yool" and "yewl" and even "Jol" or "Iol," it may have designated a heathen twelve-day feast which took place in the winter months after the ground had been covered with snow, a celebration sacred to the Goths and Saxons. Some scholars insist the word is a corruption of the Greek "joulos" which meant "hymn of joy" while others trace it back to the Latin "jubilum," which was "a rejoicing time" shared by

Roman citizens in the days of Julius Caesar, based upon the Latin word for "joy," "gaudium."

The Goths had a word for wheel, "jol," which signified the turning point of the year as far as the sun was concerned, and the modern use of the wheel symbol in almanacs could have come from that practice. In the Scandinavian countries, a jolly feast was a "yolly" feast, since the natives had a difficult time pronouncing a "j" and substituted a "y" in its place (as they still speak of "John Johnson" as "Yon Yonson"), and a time of "joy" was a time of "yoy." Naturally a midwinter festival in those northern lands was a "yoyous" or a "yolly" time, and more than likely the word "Yule" came from "yol" which was a contraction of "yolly" which meant "Joy" and "Jolly" in the first place.

A search like this leads into so many blind alleys that one is tempted to settle the matter once and for all by ascribing an English origin to the word and being done with it, proving it by telling the fanciful story of the man who said to a friend one day, as they were making plans for a Christmas celebration, "Some one will have to take the part of Santa Claus." When his friend asked, "Who'll?" (a contraction of "Who will?") the other man, in the same spirit of contraction, simply replied, "You'll!" and eventually the two-word contraction became a one-word substitution, Yule.

Be that as it may, through the years Yuletide celebrations have increased both in number and in manner, until the Christmas season covers the period which begins on the Sunday nearest St. Andrew's Day (which is always November 30), through the four Sundays of December (including St. Nicholas' Day, December 6, sometimes known as Boxing Day, from the custom of the poor people who went from house to house getting gift boxes from the rich, or "Stephening" as they called it on St. Stephen's Day, December 26, when they did the very same thing all over again) continuing on through January 6, "Twelfth Night," or "Old Christmas" or Epiphany, at which time the visit of the Magi was commemorated, and continuing until three Sundays before Ash Wednesday, which marks the beginning of Lent, forty days prior to Easter Sunday. Some of these days were holidays, others were holy days; some were celebrative, others commemorative.

Adding to the confusion is the nursery rhyme of Little Jack Horner who sat in his corner eating a Christmas pie, which, after all, was only a plum pudding, and the ceremony surrounding the bringing in of the Boar's head, complete with apple in the mouth in honor of the Oxford University student of nameless fame who was reading Aristotle while walking through a nearby forest, only to be attacked by a ferocious boar. Having no other weapon than his textbook, he hurled it into the animal's mouth, whereupon the boar, finding Aristotle as difficult to swallow as anything he had ever tasted, promptly gave up the ghost. Then we have the Waits, those singing descendants of ancient night watchmen, who became wandering minstrels, singing for gold and silver as they roamed about the streets during the weeks prior to Christmas, or entertained in court or palace for whatever the traffic would allow. The one specific date that can be authenticated is 1846, when J. C. Horsley, a British artist, prepared an original drawing for a novelty called "A Christmas Card" at the request of a fellow Englishman, Joseph Cundall, who had received the original suggestion from still another man, Sir Henry Cole. Bearing the simple but timeless inscription "Merry Christmas and A Happy New Year" over a typical family scene, this card idea swept the country, and by 1870 a London firm, Marcus Ward and Company, was doing quite a seasonal business in the new line, while a Boston firm, L. Prang and Company, pioneered in New England ten years later with similar success.

One honoree about whose life and works all too little is known is composer J. S. Pierpont, author and composer of the perenially popular "Jingle Bells." Copyrighted in 1855 as "One Horse Open Sleigh," it was published again in 1857 as "Jingle Bells." That same year Pierpont published "Little White Cottage" or "Gentle Nettie Moore" with words by Marshall Pike and music, chorus and piano accompaniment by Pierpont. We do know that he was not Rev. Dr. John Pierpont (1785-1866), renowned and eminent clergyman, hymn-writer and author, who is sometimes credited with the

Christmas ditty by those who refuse to delve deeply enough into its musical history. The preacher was the grandfather of the wealthy tycoon J. Pierpont Morgan, and no relation whatsoever to the musician of "Jingle Bells" fame. So those tales that can be traced to definite sources and those traditions that have become embellished or hoary with age, all play an important part in the season known as Advent, and the festival loved universally as Christmas, the birth of Christ. If these STORIES OF YULETIDE add to one's information, satisfy another's curiosity, and thereby make the season more inspirational, the author's purpose will be accomplished and his labors more than repaid.

ERNEST K. EMURIAN
Elm Ave Methodist Church, Portsmouth, Va.

CONTENTS

THE CHRISTMAS THAT WAS

There is laughter now in Bethlehem
  for in a cattle stall
Sleeps an infant whom the angels say
  is King and Lord of all;
There is wonder, too, in Bethlehem,
  within a mother's eyes,
Who clasps a baby to her breast
  while music fills the skies.

There is mystery in Bethlehem,
  for wise men from afar
Come riding through the narrow streets
  while following a star;
They lay their costly gifts in homage
  at the infant's feet,
And bow before the babe in whom
  the heaven and earth now meet.

The night rolls back like magic
  and the heavens are rent in twain;
Angelic legions cry "All Hail!"
  earth rings with the refrain.
Tens of thousands, tens of millions,
  like the sands that mark the sea,
From the battlements of heaven
  hail the Year of Jubilee!

THE CHRISTMAS THAT IS TO BE

There is joy in Copenhagen,
  there is laughter in Paree;
Estonians are singing hymns
  along the Baltic Sea;
Sevastopol rejoices as
  her children dance and play;
And Rotterdam rebuilds her walls
  and hails His Natal Day!

There is food for starving Athens
  and in Moscow church bells ring;
Old Notre Dame is crowded
  as Parisians hail their King!
The cloisters of Westminster
  echo hymns of joy and praise;
The Bishop of Cologne proclaims
  the hope of better days.

On the saddened face of Europe
  there is gaiety and mirth,
For angels sing of peace again
  in honoring His birth.
And plundered, helpless millions
  from their hovels in the sod
Stand enraptured as they gaze aloft
  and catch a glimpse of God!

(Written during the obliteration bombings of World War II)

A VISIT TO OBERNDORF

The Story of
SILENT NIGHT

SILENT NIGHT

Eighteen miles northwest of the city of Salzburg, Austria, straddling present-day Austrian highway #159, on the banks of the Salzach river, is the small village of Oberndorf. Nestling on a small plain in view of the snow-covered Austrian Alps, this little community has played several memorable roles in the course of its long history, for Oberndorf was the port from which the ancient Romans shipped their boat loads of salt down the Salzach River to the Danube, their so-called "white gold" dug from nearby mines that burrow deeply into the rugged mountains, which brought great fortunes to those who were able to deliver it to the far corners of the expanding empire. In later centuries, some of the village's one-thousand inhabitants proudly boasted that the salt they mined with their own hands was in great demand not only in Austria's second largest city, Linz, in the western part of the country, but also in her capital city, Vienna, on her far eastern border.

As early as the twelfth century, a Church building bespoke the Christian character of the townspeople, while succeeding generations added to the original structure and later erected newer, larger and more spacious edifices on the same familiar site, all of which sanctuaries bore the name "St. Nicholas." The Church building which eventually came to be recognized as the town's most famous landmark was erected sometime during the middle ages, and was a combination of Gothic, Romanesque and Byzantine architecture. Situated on a small alley between the town's principal thoroughfare and the rushing waters of the Salzach river, the building rose to a height of thirty feet, while its square tower, topped with a triple-tiered bulbous steeple, that gave striking evidence of the Turkish occupation of the territory prior to their defeat before the walls of Vienna and their eventual return to their own borders, was visible for miles around. This Turkish, Moorish or Byzantine style of architecture is still a striking characteristic of those large public buildings of western Austria that have survived the ravages of time and the destruction of numerous European wars.

The name of the "patron saint" of the local congregation was an appropriate one, for the villagers had heard of many leading seaport cities scattered throughout Italy and Greece that had adopted Nicholas as their very own, regarding him as both the official and unofficial guardian of travellers by land and sea. Nicholas came by his fame justly, for, as the renowned Christian Bishop of Myra in Asia Minor during the fourth century of the Christian era, he had been the defender and protector of many wayfarers, both men and women, as well as the confidant and companion of the small children of his parish. As the fame of his charitable deeds was carried by word of mouth from town to town and city to city, others sought his guardianship. Later, after he had been canonized by the Roman Catholic Church, the sixth of December became known as "St. Nicholas' Day," and those who feared robbers by land or pirates by sea called upon him to watch over them during their perilous journeys and bring them safely to their desired havens. The three gold balls with which the kindly Bishop dispensed his charities were so closely identified with the man himself that a friend made a sign bearing facsimiles of those three balls of gold to signify the place where the good Churchman distributed his alms to those in need. During the middle ages some financial wizards who were anxious to make their fortunes by lending money at exorbitant rates of interest adopted his sign of the three gold balls, hoping that those who wanted aid would see the sign, come into their shops and borrow what they needed at rates of interest determined by the money-lending pawn brokers themselves.

As the practise of celebrating the birth of Our Lord in late December spread from Christian country to Christian country, children as well as adults began to speak of St.

Nicholas as the person who distributed gifts on Christmas Eve, and some who did not connect the name with the actual historical person, and others who considered him merely a legendary figure whose reality was shrouded in the mists of history attributed to this St. Nicholas, shortened conveniently to St. Nick, all of the good things that were associated with the Advent season. As the legend grew and spread to more distant lands, St. Nick became known as Santa Claus, and it was later deemed an act of providence that those who began the Church at Oberndorf selected Nicholas as their personal patron, naming their Church in his honor.

Through the centuries the town grew very slowly. It was not until the year 1540 that a square stone water tower about one-hundred feet high was erected some twenty-five yards nearer the banks of the river than the property on which the most recent Church building had been erected. Again, it was later regarded as more than a mere accident that a first and only son was born to an Oberndorf couple, Franz and Anna Mohr, on December 11, 1792, the month set aside for the celebration of The Lord's birthday. The father, Franz, an old-style soldier of fortune, had been "a roving mercenary musketeer" who fought in the army that paid him the best, serving for some years in the military forces of the Archbishop of Salzburg. Due to his long absences from home in obedience to his orders as a soldier, the young lad soon found himself under the tutelage of a Catholic priest, Father Hiernle, who became his foster father as well. Christened in the Church of St. Nicholas, he was given the surname Joseph, a name selected by his parents from the Biblical husband of Mary and the earthly father of Jesus.

Since the village offered few opportunities for commercial advancement and almost none whatsoever for a growing boy who needed an education, the Mohrs moved eighteen miles south to the city of Salzburg, occupying the humble house at Number Nine, Stein Gasser (Stone Street), a little narrow cobble-stone street not more than ten feet wide. Its only redeeming feature was the fact that the Mohr dwelling fronted on another equally narrow street that led directly to the rushing waters of the Salzach less than a hundred yards away. Years later the pupils of the Middle School (Gymnasium) of Salzburg raised money and placed a plaque on the bare cement front of that small building, bearing the inscription: "In this house Joseph Mohr, 1792-1848, the author of the song Silent Night, was brought and spent his childhood years."

One year before Joseph's birth, Salzburg's most illustrious man of genius, Wolfgang Amadeus Mozart (1756-1791), had died, but already the four-story house on the opposite side of the river where the brilliant composer had been born, and the larger, more comfortable home to which he and his family had moved in the newer section of the city, just a couple blocks from the Mohr's new residence, and where the youth had composed some of his noblest works, were being pointed out as famous shrines and visited by those who had either heard or heard of the city's most renowned citizen. Doubtless Joseph Mohr, too, along with his boyhood chums or classmates, climbed the flights of stairs to inspect the small rooms of the composer's birthplace across the river, or visited the second floor apartment of his later residence to strike some random chords on Mozart's piano, or to see some of his original manuscripts or marvel at the assortment of orchestral instruments for which he had composed some of his most brilliant works.

At that time it is unlikely that Joseph had ever heard of another Austrian youth, a school teacher and composer-to-be by the name of Franz Gruber, who had been born in the town of Hallein, some ten miles south of Salzburg, on November 25, 1787. It is more likely that Franz visited Salzburg and possibly passed Joseph on one of the narrow crowded streets than that Joseph ever went to Hallein, the site of one of Austria's most productive and most lucrative salt mines, to encounter the lad with whom he was eventually to collaborate in producing one of Christendom's loveliest Christmas carols. Possibly Franz, the third son of a poor weaver, as a growing boy, came often to Salzburg with his parents, since it was the largest city in that section, not only to shop in the stores and the market place, but also to marvel at the magnificence of the huge castle that towered over the city and to climb the steep hill and visit the small but superbly constructed "stone city" that was one of the city's famed landmarks. The two boys may have huffed and puffed their way up the narrow path, through a series of guarding gates with their portcullises still intact, to view the city from the topmost tower or to stand in awe before the suits of armor that heralded the bygone days of chivalry and knighthood, without ever knowing that God in His divine providence had destined them to meet sooner than they expected, if not in the thriving cultured city of Salzburg, then in the small, obscure, relatively unimportant town of Oberndorf, eighteen miles north. The salt mine at Hallein was equally as famous and as important as the ones nearer Oberndorf for many years, but, as the veins of salt near the northern village began to run out, miners began discovering larger veins in the areas to the south, and soon the authorities were concentrating their efforts at Hallein where larger yields produced larger profits, than in the north where smaller yields prophesied shrinking dividends. When Joseph finished his preliminary education in the local schools, he felt the call to the ministry of his Church. Although at one time, Salzburg had been a strong and vigorous Protestant city following the Lutheran Reformation in the early sixteenth century, the Roman Catholic Church, in the violent excesses of its Counter-reformation, selected this city as one of its principal targets, and, with a fearfulness that belied its profession to be acting in the spirit of Christ, wrought such persecutions among the Protestants and pursued its aim of completely destroying them with such tyrannical vigor and maniacal fury that, almost over night, Salzburg became a Roman Catholic stronghold once more, a character which it bears to this day. It was under the influence of Father Hiernle that young Joseph embraced the priesthood at the age of twenty-two, on August 21, 1815, and embarked upon his life's work. Thus it came to pass that, after serving in a variety of priestly capacities in several parishes in the diocese of Salzburg, Father Mohr, at the age of twenty-six, in the year 1818, was the assistant parish priest at the Church of St. Nicholas in his own native village of Oberndorf, a position he occupied for only two years, from 1817 to 1819.

As for Franz Gruber of Hallein, he had, despite the objections of his poor father who considered a musical career an invitation to more abject poverty than his own, taught himself to play the violin, and later studied with a well known organ professor at Burghausen, George Hartdobler. When he discovered that his salary as a school teacher was hardly more than a pitiful pittance, Gruber applied for the position as organist and choir master in several nearby Churches, soon playing the pipe organs and directing the choirs in Oberndorf and nearby Armsdorf. With no illusions of ever becoming a "second Mozart," Franz pursued his musical career and assumed the responsibilities of his two parishes with a sense of devotion that had in it none of the urgency that drives a genius to express himself creatively or perish!

Christmas Eve that year, 1818, was not much different from many other Christmas Eves, save for the fact that Joseph and Franz were now mature men and faced the season rather philosophically instead of with the eager expectancy of childhood or the wide-eyed wonder of early adolescence. However, there was much to be thankful for this particular Christmas, for Napoleon was still safely out of the way, having been banished to the lonely island of St. Helena three years before, after the debacle at Waterloo in 1815. Many townspeople recalled the Christmas when "The Little Corporal" had billeted his army in their houses and huts on his way to assault Salzburg and attack Vienna. In fact, most of them had seen the very cannon ball that had penetrated the outer wall of Salzburg Castle and brought about its humiliating capitulation. But now that was past, and a semblance of peace and order had supplanted the Frenchman's wild dreams of world conquest and personal glory. When Franz Gruber tried out the pipe organ in Joseph's Church that morning, he was surprised to find the instrument in worse condition than it had been in many years. The church mice had chewed so many large holes in the bellows, and gnawed so many leather connections to bits that the instrument refused to respond to his artistry, and the musician rather dolefully faced the prospect of a Midnight Mass without any instrumental music whatsoever. When he conveyed his dismay to the parish priest, Mohr refused to become alarmed or unduly upset, and just said, "Franz, do the best you can with what you have," a statement that would have riled a man of less composure since he had already done just exactly that! Undaunted but discouraged, he went back to try to work a miracle in a place where miracles are often needed but seldom performed, and sweated out a few more hours on the decrepit old instrument. Meantime, Father Mohr visited some of the needy families in his expanding parish, distributing food and clothing and gifts, walking through the heavy snow to the center of the village and then trudging through the fields back of the Church to bless a baby that had recently been born into one of the poorer families on the outskirts of the town. When he coupled his personal experiences with that of the birth of Jesus in a distant country centuries earlier, he was moved to express his convictions and emotions in a very simple original religious poem of three stanzas of five lines each. As translated literally, and not poetically, from Mohr's actual German stanzas, the poem, entitled "Stille Nacht" (Silent Night) contained these lines:

Silent night, holy night,
Everyone sleeps; only the lonely ones are awake,
The pious and blessed couple
Who were in Bethlehem's stable
With the heavenly child.

Silent night, holy night,
Shepherds were the first to get the news;
Through the angel's hallelujah
It resounds with rejoicing far and near,
Christ the Saviour is here.

Silent night, holy night;
Son of God; oh, how he smiles lovely
Out of his most gracious mouth
When the saving hour strikes for us,
Christ, in your birth.

When Franz Gruber entered Mohr's home a short while later in complete disgust and disappointment at being unable to repair the pipe organ, Joseph merely smiled at him, handed him an old guitar and a copy of his new stanzas and said, "If you cannot play the organ, then compose some music for my new poem and you can play it on the guitar while we sing it as a duet tonight."

Too flabbergasted to object, Gruber strummed three chords on the guitar, and began humming an appropriate melody as he read through the new stanzas. The only change or alteration he made in his friend's poem was to repeat the last line, since his melody reached its climax on that line and needed a closing phrase to resolve itself and bring the tune to a fitting conclusion. At Midnight Mass, on Christmas Eve 1818, Franz played the guitar while he and Joseph sang their new carol for the worshippers who crowded the Church of St. Nicholas for that colorful, inspiring and traditional service. While they liked it and commented favorably to both the poet and composer, they little dreamed that one day the village of Oberndorf would become as famous a shrine as the birthplace of Mozart in nearby Salzburg.

When Karl Mauracher, an organ builder and repairman from the Zillertal Valley farther east finally reached Oberndorf to fix the broken down pipe organ the following spring, Mohr insisted that Gruber play the new carol for their visitor on the rebuilt instrument. Gruber finally yielded to Mohr's insistence, as a result of which Mauracher was equally insistent that he be given a manuscript copy of the song by the composer himself, a request Gruber could not well refuse. It was Mauracher who taught the song to the four Strasser children back in his native valley in the Tyrolean region of Austria, and it was these four singing children, Caroline, Joseph, Andreas and Amalie, who renamed it "The Song From Heaven" and sang it publicly at the great fair in Leipzig to attract customers to their parents' booth where Father and Mother Strasser had some of their handmade choice chamois skin gloves on display and for sale. At the invitation of the Director-General of Music for the Kingdom of Saxony, the four children sang their new song for the

King and Queen in the Royal Saxon Court Chapel in Pleissenburg Castle that same year, on Christmas Eve, 1832. Later, when King William IV of Prussia heard it, he expressed the desire that "Stille Nacht" be given first place in all future Christmas concerts within the bounds of his domain. If Mohr ever penned another Christmas poem of equal beauty or if Gruber ever composed a melody as sweet and as lovely, neither has ever come to light.

The priest fulfilled his ministry to the best of his ability and as ably as he could, serving many parishes in the diocese of Salzburg, dying thirty years after writing his most famous poem, and just six days prior to his fifty-sixth birthday, passing away on December 5, 1848 at Wagram, the village near Vienna made famous by Napoleon's crushing defeat of the Austrian army there in July, 1809. As for Franz Gruber, he composed nearly a hundred sacred songs and served various Churches as organist and choir master until his death at the age of seventy-eight on July 7, 1865, his last position, a choral directorship in his native Hallein, lasting for thirty-two years, from 1833 until 1865. While Mohr went back to his birthplace at Oberndorf to write his finest poem, Gruber went back to his birthplace, Hallein, twenty-eight miles from the scene of his greatest creative triumph, to serve his longest tenure and there to die and be buried. A letter in the handwriting of Franz Gruber, dated December 30, 1854, and now a prized possession of the Hallein Museum, authenticates the story of the part he and Father Mohr played in giving the world this matchlessly beautiful Christmas carol.

The Salzach River runs fast and swiftly from the snow capped Alps down through the valley southward, as it passes many stagnant villages like Oberndorf and a growing city like Salzburg before emptying into the Danube (which the Austrians call "The Donau"), eventually finding its way to the Black Sea. Occasionally when the snows of winter are heavier than usual and the spring thaws come with greater rapidity, the Salzach becomes a raging torrent, tearing down from its mountain heights to overflow the valleys below and inundate towns and cities with no respect of person, place or thing, destroying home, school, church and prison alike in its downward plunge toward the Danube. While numerous floods had swept over the region during the seventeenth and early eighteenth centuries, none had caused the widespread damage or wrought the havoc that a series of violent floods in 1896, 1897 and 1899 left in their wake. In some places the rushing river rose fifteen to twenty feet above normal, sweeping away buildings of all sizes and descriptions, and increasing the destruction farther down the river as buildings smashed into buildings, and huge trees, like gigantic battering rams, beat against formidable structures until they, too, tumbled over and were washed away. What the floods of those years did not succeed in claiming, the floods of 1913 did. To this day photographs of the overflowing river that covered the business and residential areas on either side of the Salzach in Salzburg hang from the walls of many public buildings as grim reminders of the damage such a flood can possibly bring once more upon an unprepared citizenry. During the floods of 1896-1899, sections of the Church of St. Nicholas in Oberndorf were severely affected and one corner of the large structure dangerously undermined. It was not, however, until the climactic floods of 1913 that the Church building was actually endangered. The waters seemed angrier and more demanding than ever that year, as they beat against the historic sanctuary, and rose to such frightening proportions that they even overflowed the altar of the Church itself, washing away much of the foundation and superstructure on one side of the towering edifice. It was then that the townspeople, now numbering some three-thousand, decided that the time had finally come when they had to move their Church to a safer, higher site on the opposite side of the river at the far end of their small community. While the Church had been badly battered by the large trees the river had uprooted high in the mountains, the ancient stone water tower nearby survived the ravages, and, when the waters finally subsided, it was found to be as stable and as strong as the day it had been completed nearly four centuries earlier. To this day, townspeople point to the marks of the high water on the outside of this water tower, as well as on one or two barns and dwellings that endured the watery onslaughts without being destroyed. Meantime, the altar of the old Church was preserved, to become a permanent part of a new building, whenever and wherever it would be completed. The ancient tracker action pipe organ, whose breakdown had occasioned the writing of "Silent Night" was dismantled and moved to a Church nearer Salzburg where it is still in constant use after the passing of so many memorable decades. When the new Church was finally completed, it was a large, handsome, imposing structure, topped with a conventional Gothic pointed steeple above the traditional square tower, the architectural styles of the east finally giving way to those of the west. The name attached to the new building was, of course, "The Church of St. Nicholas." After the last stone of the famous old building had been removed and the last bit of dirt shovelled in place to even up the yard and smooth over the areas on which the older structure had stood for so many generations, it suddenly dawned upon some of the friends of the Church and community that the spot made sacred by "Silent Night" was as worthy of being commemorated and perpetuated as was the birthplace of Mozart in Salzburg. Under the leadership and inspiration of a group of interested Austrians, steps were immediately taken to erect a suitable shrine on the site of the old Church, the actual planning and construction being undertaken during the years 1924-1936, under the guidance of Professor Keldorfer, the government official in charge of historical monuments for that section of the country. Assisting him were other men whose names were later inscribed upon a plaque inside the completed building: the Lord Mayor or Burgomaster, Anton Pfoss; a priest, R. Max Fellacher; another priest, Math. Gumpold; two teachers, F. Schmidmeier and Frz. Schwenke; a Police Inspector, Josef Percht, and Frz. Armsdorfer, while J. Dietzinger served as the architect for the project. As a result of their combined endeavours, on the acre of ground formerly occupied by the well-known historic Church, a small octagonal chapel was erected, topped with a rounded dome roof and an open eight-sided cupola in place of a tower or steeple, with a small stoop facing the alley-way that led from the main street to the river, the main structure being finished with stucco on the outside as are most Austrian homes, churches and public buildings. To safeguard this chapel from the ravages of future floods, a mound of dirt some eight feet high and twenty-five feet square was placed near the center of the large lot and anchored with stones and protected with strong hedges, before the foundation for the new chapel was laid and the building undertaken. Adorned as well as decorated with stained glass windows honoring both Mohr and Gruber, this chapel is the scene of an annual pilgrimage on Christmas Eve when townspeople re-enact the famous incidents of 1818, taking the roles of the priest and the musician as they dramatize the events that inspired the writing of "Silent Night." The brass band from the local school and members of the school chorus and community choir always look forward to participating in this Advent festival of song and story.

The area surrounding this lovely picturesque chapel is protected by a five-foot hedge of evergreens, while chickens from nearby farms feed on the grass among the thirteen trees as their ancestors must have done in bygone days. Nine magnificent seventy-foot cedars, two beautiful forty-foot high silver spruce and two back yard poplars add a solemnity to the scene. Eleven steps bring one to the porch of the tiny memorial while two more lead up to the inside of the building itself. When the chapel was finally finished and the new memorial stained glass picture windows by Tirolier Glasmalerei of Innsbruck were installed, permission was granted the sponsors to go to the grave of Joseph Mohr in Wagram and bring back his skull and bury it in the cement that holds up the altar of the shrine that commemorates his Christian hymn. The altar itself is made up of a large wood carving, the principal center section showing the traditional Christmas scene of the birth of Our Lord in the manger at Bethlehem, while the three smaller sections beneath the main panel depict the visit of the Magi, the Lord's crucifixion, and the flight into Egypt. While this is not a Church in the strict sense of the word, one Mass is said in the chapel annually, during the commemorative rites every Christmas Eve. Although the four small plain wooden pews, two on each side with a protective railing in front and kneeling benches underneath, can accommodate only ten or fifteen worshippers at a time, visitors take turns reading the inscriptions and sitting or kneeling in prayer in the benches or on the stone floor. Some even bring flowers or descriptive banners to hang beneath Gruber's or Mohr's memorial windows to signify their gratitude for the song the men were privileged to write, while others, individually or in small groups, sing "Silent Night" in hushed reverence as they think back to the memorable events of the preceding century. Fittingly, the inscription on the only door to the memorial contains this Biblical promise, first spoken by the angels to the wondering shepherds that first Christmas, "Peace to men on earth who have goodwill." While many of the townspeople commute to Salzburg every day, or make gloves within the confines of their own little village as their ancestors had been doing for untold generations, the new Church of St. Nicholas continues to be the center of their lives.

"Silent Night" might have been lost to the outside world had it not been for the brilliant scholarship of an American Episcopalian Bishop whose exquisite rendition of Mohr's stanzas into the English language made the hymn available to a larger and more appreciative audience. Rev. John Freeman Young (1820-1885) in 1863, four years prior to his elevation to the episcopacy of his denomination, discovered "Silent Night" and decided it was worth translating into his own tongue, a labor of love that has put English-speaking Christendom in his debt. Until exhaustive research by another Episcopalian rector, Rev. Byron Edward Underwood of Massachusetts, the name of the translator had been unknown or forgotten. The artistry with which the future bishop approached this difficult task may be seen when one compares his version with that of the literal English translation of Mohr's three original stanzas, for it was Rev. J. F. Young, future Bishop of Florida, who made the Austrian priest sing:

Silent night, holy night,
All is calm, all is bright;
Round yon, Virgin Mother and child,
Holy infant so tender and mild,
Sleep in heavenly peace.

Silent night, holy night,
Shepherds quake at the sight;
Glories stream from heaven afar;
Heavenly hosts sing "Alleluia,
Christ the Saviour is born."

Silent night, holy night;
Son of God, love's pure Light
Radiant beams from Thy holy face,
With the dawn of redeeming grace,
Jesus, Lord, at Thy birth.

Since Mohr only wrote three stanzas, undoubtedly the fourth and final stanza of Bishop Young's version was his very own, for in none of the manuscripts or faithful copies thereof does Father Mohr mention "the star," of which the American divine sang in his closing lines:

Silent night, holy night,
Wondrous star, lend thy light;
With the angels let us sing
Alleluia to our King;
Christ the Saviour is born.

JOURNEY IN DECEMBER

Rich men journey to New York,
  prospectors to Nome;
Men of science go to London,
  men of art to Rome.
Men who worship pleasure
  go to gay Paree;
Men who love adventure go
  to Suez by the sea.

Rulers go to Washington,
  doctors to Berlin;
Radicals to Leningrad,
  singers to Turin.
Mighty cities: Monuments
  glorifying men.
Only wise ones see a star
  and go to Bethlehem.

THE STORIES OF THREE CHRISTMAS HYMNS

Thou Didst Leave Thy Throne
O Come, O Come, Immanuel
In The Bleak Mid-Winter

THOU DIDST LEAVE THY THRONE

The poor innkeeper at Bethlehem that first Christmas Eve has come in for a lot of criticism in the intervening centuries, ever since the author of the third Gospel included this brief statement as an appendage to the narrative of the Christ Child's birth, "And she brought forth her first born son and wrapped him in swaddling clothes and laid him in a manger; because there was no room for them in the inn" (Luke 2:7).

Despite the fact that little Bethlehem was crowded to capacity with many weary and worn travellers from the far distances of the Roman empire who had made the perilous journey in obedience to the decree of Emperor Caesar Augustus that "the whole world should be taxed," a rather heartless imperial command that necessitated the return of every taxable adult to the place of his birth, the innkeeper is the one who has been maligned, castigated, rebuked, ridiculed, misunderstood and held up before the world as a money-hungry heartless businessman who had no consideration whatsoever for the Holy Family on the night which was to see the Virgin Mother bring forth her first born son. The few known facts of the case are somewhat different and rather alarmingly simple. Joseph and Mary were by no means the earliest arrivals at the City of David that busy day, and by the time they reached the outskirts of the little village it was no doubt long past the noonday hour and rapidly approaching the time of the evening meal. The owners and managers of the few scattered hostels could hardly be blamed for operating their establishments on a "first come, first served" basis for as yet no Heavenly messenger or Angel from the Lord had forewarned any of them to be on the lookout for a "woman great with child" and her husband, an humble carpenter from far off Nazareth, and keep a room in reserve for them.

When Joseph knocked at the innkeeper's door, no doubt every available sleeping spot had been sold out for hours, if not for days, and there is hardly any doubt that the owner himself had squeezed his own large family into one or two small rooms in order to accommodate as many out-of-towners as he could during those exciting days, a tribute to his compassion as well as to his resourcefulness. After all, it is not every day in the year or every year in a decade that the Emperor orders such a migration of citizens for the purpose of a joint census and taxing, and if Bethlehem was bursting at the seams that night, it was Caesar's fault, not the innkeeper's! Most of those who came into town late in the afternoon or early in the evening usually managed to find shelter in the home of a distant relative or a close friend, and doubtless many who returned to Bethlehem in obedience to the Augustan order did just that, making out best they could under the peculiar circumstances. As for the innkeeper, he was merely doing his job to the best of his limited ability under most trying conditions, and if St. Luke just had not mentioned the fact that "there was no room in the inn," this man would have gone to his reward feeling that he had done more than his share in providing Joseph and Mary with a warm dry spot in the barn back of the main establishment where, in the presence of the silent sheep and the lowing kine, she gave birth to the Son of God.

While the third evangelist's brief statement has been the inspiration for many a fanciful tale during the last two millenia, it has inspired very few hymns, for there is nothing hymnic or romantic about an innkeeper who is so cruel and heartless that he has no place inside the inn for the birth of the Messiah. Such a man generally merits the vitriolic condemnation of the novelist, short-story writer, poet and caustic critic, if he actually was as bad a man as he has been pictured. Little wonder then that few hymn writers have discovered any virtues worth extolling in a hymn of praise in this man's experience, or sung of his unselfishness in a poem by means of which others could worship God in the years ahead. The one poet who not only attempted this task but did a remarkably successful job of it was Emily Elizabeth Steele Elliott (1836-1897) a brilliant British woman of letters whose aunt, Charlotte Elliott (1789-1871) earned world-wide fame for her beautiful autobiographical hymn "Just As I Am, Without One Plea," penned the year of her niece's birth. But Emily, the talented third daughter of an Anglican clergyman and distinguished author, Rev. Edward B. Elliott, pastor of St. Mark's Church, Brighton, England, wasted little of her poetic skill lambasting the innkeeper or enumerating his evident vices in the custom of the day. The twenty-eight year old editor and poet, looking beyond the obvious details of the Biblical story, and recalling the admonition of St. Paul to the Church at Ephesus "that Christ may dwell in your hearts by faith" (Ephesians 3:17) made her poem a prayer that Christ, denied a room in Bethlehem, would come to her heart and abide there, concluding the first four of her five stanzas with this deeply revealing invitation, "O come to my heart, Lord Jesus, There is room in my heart for Thee." Then, instead of confining her hymn to the events surrounding the Advent season, she studied the Gospel narratives and included in her stanzas references to others who, in addition to the innkeeper, had had no room for the Lord, making of her hymn more than a Christmas carol whose use would be limited to the twelfth month of the year, but more of a general hymn on the life and victory of her Lord, which could be used as a paean of praise the whole year through. In a poetic meter that allowed the writer unusual freedom of expression and was therefore called "irregular," Emily Elliott told her story in these descriptive lines:

Thou didst leave Thy throne and Thy kingly crown When
Thou camest to earth for me;
But in Bethlehem's home there was found no room for Thy
holy nativity.
O come to my heart, Lord Jesus, There is room in my heart
for Thee.

Heaven's arches rang when the angels sang Proclaiming Thy royal degree;
But in lowly birth didst Thou come to earth, And in great humility.
O come to my heart, Lord Jesus, There is room in my heart for Thee.

The foxes found rest and the birds their nest In the shade of the forest tree;
But Thy couch was the sod, O Thou Son of God In the deserts of Galilee.
O come to my heart, Lord Jesus, There is room in my heart for Thee.

Thou camest, O Lord, with the living Word That should set Thy people free;
But with mocking scorn and with crown of thorn, They bore Thee to Calvary.
O come to my heart, Lord Jesus, There is room in my heart for Thee.

When heaven's arches ring and her choirs shall sing At Thy coming to victory,
Let Thy voice call me home, saying "Yet there is room,
There is room at My side for thee."
And my heart shall rejoice, Lord Jesus, When Thou comest and callest for me.

First printed privately for the children and young people of her father's Brighton parish, Emily's hymn was included the following year, 1865, in "Service of Praise," a collection of hymns and sacred songs edited by a Mr. Wilson. The author herself later included the hymn in the 1870 edition of "The Church Missionary Juvenile Instructor" which she edited for several years and in the 1880 edition of her collection, "Chimes for Daily Service." Of her nearly one-hundred-fifty hymns, this one alone outgrew the scenes of its birth and became worldwide in its influence.

Like her distinguished aunt Charlotte, Emily never married but she was still privileged to live a life of great usefulness, giving herself to many causes connected with the advancement of the Kingdom of God, particularly the Mildmay Park missionary project.

Twelve years after Miss Elliott wrote her hymn, Rev. Timothy Matthews (1826-1910), a British clergyman who made more of a name for himself as an organist and composer than a preacher or pastor, set her stanzas to music, naming his original tune "Margaret" (from a Greek word meaning "pearl"), deviating from the general practice of naming tunes after significant places, or from one of the names of the author or composer. For that reason the music sometimes goes by the name of "Elliott" after Miss Emily herself, as well as by "Margaret" which was chosen by the composer for reasons best known to himself which he never cared to reveal to the curious public. In the 1954 edition of the official British Methodist Hymnal, three Matthews' tunes are included, "Margaret," "Saxby" composed in 1883, and "North Coates" while the 1951 edition of "Congregational Praise," published for the Congregational Union of England and Wales, a monumental collection of more than one-thousand hymns, lists two more, "Corfe Mullen" and "Ludborough." Of Emily's stanzas and Timothy's one-hundred or more hymn tunes, only "Thou Didst Leave Thy Throne" have proved acceptable to American Christians, and the passing of time only increases its popularity, as it is generally considered now one of the finest hymns dealing with both the birth, life, death and triumph of Our Lord. If it can continue to remind believers of all ages that Christ is always seeking an abiding place in each individual heart, its ministry will be an effective and worthwhile one in every way.

O COME, O COME, IMMANUEL

A study of the Holy Bible reveals that God's relationship to His people is threefold: 1. God the Father is God For Us, a conviction and doctrine clearly expressed by the New Testament writers in such familiar passages as Romans 8:31, "If God be for us, who can be against us?", Romans 5:8, "But God commendeth his love toward us in that, while we were yet sinners, Christ died for us"; I Corinthians 11:24, "Take, eat, this is my body which is broken for you"; I Timothy 2:5-6, "The man Christ Jesus, who gave himself a ransom for all"; Titus 2:13-14, "Jesus Christ who gave himself for us"; Galatians 2:20, "The life which I now live in the flesh I live by faith in the Son of God who loved me and gave himself for me." That God is truly on the side of His people is borne out by the use of the words "us," "all" and "me" in these quotations. 2. God the Son is God With Us, a mutual relationship seen in Enoch walking with God (Genesis 5:22) and in Isaiah's prophecy of the coming king found in Isaiah 7:14, "Therefore the Lord himself shall give you a sign. Behold the virgin shall conceive and bear a son and shall call his name Immanuel," and quoted by the author of the first Gospel in Matthew 1:22-23. Using the same word and idea in another place, Isaiah 8:8 stated that "the stretching out of his wings shall fill the breadth of thy land, O Immanuel," while Isaiah 8:10 warned the enemies of Israel, "Take counsel together and it shall come to nought; speak the word and it shall not stand, for God is with us!" 3. God the Holy Ghost or the Holy Spirit is God In Us. Paul climaxed his personal witness with this affirmation in Galatians 2:20, "I am crucified with Christ; nevertheless I live; yet not I but Christ liveth in me." He prayed for the Church at Ephesus "that Christ may dwell in your hearts by faith" (Ephesians 3:17) while he exhorted the Romans "But ye are not in the flesh but in the Spirit, if so be that the Spirit of God dwell in you" (Romans 8:9 and 11). Furthermore, Paul asked the Church at Corinth, "Know ye not that ye are the temple of God, and that the Spirit of God dwelleth in you?" (I Corinthians 3:17). Speaking of the promised Comforter, the Spirit of truth, Jesus told His disciples, "for he dwelleth with you and shall be in you" (John 4:17) while John himself later wrote in his letters, "By this we know that we abide in him and he in us, because he has given us of his Spirit" (I

John 4:13) and "Whosoever shall confess that Jesus is the Son of God, God dwelleth in him and he in God" (I John 4:15) and "God is love; and he that dwelleth in love dwelleth in God and God in him" (I John 4:16). It was this third relationship that inspired Rev. Phillips Brooks (1835-1893) the future Bishop of the Episcopal Church in Massachusetts to include this closing prayer in his lovely Christmas carol "O Little Town Of Bethlehem,"

> O Holy Child of Bethlehem, Descend to us, we pray;
> Cast out our sin and enter in, Be born in us today.

But it was the second relationship contained in the Hebrew word "Immanuel" which inspired Rev. John Mason Neale, the brilliant British Anglican divine, to give Christendom one of her most unusual and plaintive Christmas hymns, one he rendered into the English language "O Come, O Come, Immanuel."

Isaiah, one of the major prophets of Old Testament times, delivered some of his most forceful prophecies during the reign of Ahaz, King of the southern province of Judah for sixteen years, 741-726 B.C. So utterly different was this wicked ruler from his father, that he turned against the advice and warnings of the elders and re-introduced the pagan worship of Baal and Moloch, even going so far as to offer his own two sons as burnt sacrifices to these tribal deities. Attacked on all sides by his enemies, the Syrians, the Edomites, the Israelites and Philistines, he saw the fortunes of Judah fall to a low ebb during his reign. According to Isaiah's account of these tragic times, God spoke to Ahaz in his capital city, Jerusalem, saying, "Ask a sign of the Lord thy God; ask it, either in the depth or in the height above" to which the evil monarch replied, "I will not ask neither will I tempt the Lord." It was then that the prophet uttered the majestic words that contained the promise of an eventual deliverer, later recorded in Isaiah 4:7, quoted above. Succeeding verses spoke of the judgment God would mete out upon the land of Judah at the hands of the armies of the Assyrians to the east, but the significance of this passage consists in the fact that the name "Immanuel" appears here for the first time in Holy

Writ, its only other appearance among the thirty-nine books of the Old Testament being in the previously quoted threat found in Isaiah 8:8. Of all the names ascribed to the coming Messiah, Immanuel is not only the most musical but also the most beautiful, for it means "God With Us."

Centuries after Isaiah spoke his comforting words to a distraught, discouraged and divided people, Matthew, the first of the four evangelists, applied those very same words to the person of Jesus, seeing in the birth of Christ their actual historical fulfilment, including in his narrative the New Testament application of the Old Testament proclamation, "Now all this was done that it might be fulfilled which was spoken of the Lord by the prophet, Behold a virgin shall be with child and shall bring forth a son and they shall call his name Emmanuel, which, being interpreted is, God with us" (Matthew 1:22-23). Isaiah spelled the word with an "I" and Matthew with an "E" but the basic meaning of the word was in no way affected or altered. The recent controversy over the Revised Standard Version's substitution of the phrase "a young woman" in Isaiah's prophecy for the Authorized Version's word "virgin" was absolutely unnecessary since the original Hebrew word referred to a young woman of marriageable age, which in the orient of Isaiah's day naturally presupposed virginity. That it may not do so in the twentieth century is more of a reflection upon the loose morals of our own generation than upon the scholarship of the translators of this latest English version of The Holy Bible. Although in other portions of his writings, Isaiah spoke of the coming deliverer as the suffering servant, the wonderful counsellor, the mighty God, the everlasting father and the prince of peace, it was Immanuel that became the most endearing term, passing from the Hebrew of Isaiah through the Greek of Matthew into the Latin of Jerome and early Christendom.

During the tenth and eleventh centuries of the Christian era, the antiphonal style of singing came into full fruition, with hymns, psalms and responses being sung back and forth or alternately by two choirs on either side of the chancel or even at either end of the main section of the church or cathedral, rather than in unison by the combined choirs singing simultaneously. Sometimes the precentor or leader would sing one line, the response being sung by the choir or by the entire assembled congregation. As this custom spread and variations developed in different centers of religious and musical culture, a series of such antiphonal songs evolved that became known as Antiphons, songs of praise or response composed to be sung antiphonally for certain services of worship or at particular seasons of the year or during special religious celebrations. Since seven of the more important or prominent or popular antiphonal compositions all began with the Latin word "O," they began to be known as the "Seven O's" rather than the "Seven Greater Antiphons." During the thirteenth century some unknown scholar and choral arranger fashioned these "Seven O's" into one long Latin hymn of seven stanzas. When these antiphons were sung in public, usually important personages or those who occupied official positions in the respective monasteries or cathedrals were selected to sing the seven different parts or stanzas of the hymn, and it was considered an honor for a man to be chosen to sing one of the antiphons during a particular religious exercise at a special festival or service of worship. The "Seven Greater Antiphons" began with the Latin phrases O Sapientia (O Wisdom), Adonai (O Lord), O Radix Jesse (O root of Jesse), O Clavis David (O Key of David), O Oriens (O Orient), O Rex (O King), and O Emmanuel (O God With Us).

Of course there were many editions and variations of these responses, but generally those that were sung or chanted in connection with the reading of the Old Testament Psalms or the New Testament lessons (particularly the Magnificat, Mary's song of praise that begins "My soul doth magnify the Lord") on the four Sundays of the Advent season immediately prior to Christmas Day itself, followed this pattern.

Dr. John Mason Neale, the renowned English clergyman whose brilliant translations of early Greek and Latin hymns filled fifteen volumes of published works "that were incomparably superior to that of any other translator," in his exhaustive research into the backgrounds and original writings of the monks and martyrs who were the original hymn writers of their day, discovered one version of the seventh antiphon

"O Emmanuel" which began "Veni, Veni, Immanuel." In addition, he learned that by the time this adaptation of the response came into common use, it was being sung to the haunting minor strains of a typical thirteenth century plainsong, the tune being by no means a new one but rather a combination of familiar phrases from older Latin Masses that had been effected by several unknown composers and editors during the previous century.

Neale (1818-1866) who was unable to accept one or two fairly respectable appointments in the Anglican Church because of ill-health, finally ended up as the warden of Sackville College, an humble church-endowed alms house some twenty-five miles from London, a place he filled with pioneering fortitude for twenty years, during which he gave Christendom some of her best gems of original writing, editing and translating, among his works being some of the noblest hymns in the English language. Unappreciated by several of his pompous ecclesiastical superiors and doomed to spend his most creative and productive years as the spiritual father of a handful of aged cast-aways, Neale lost no time in weeping or feeling sorry for himself but buried himself in the creative work he loved, as one result of which he was inspired to poetize the seven great antiphons and give the Church one of her most unusual Christmas hymns. Making the last response of the Latin the first in his English rendition, and adapting the rest for general use, Neale wrote, among others, these stanzas:

O come, O come, Immanuel, And ransome captive Israel,
That mourns in lonely exile here, Until the Son of God appear.
Chorus: Rejoice! Rejoice! Immanuel shall come to thee, O Israel.

O come, O come, Thou Lord of might, Who to Thy tribes on Sinai's height,
In ancient times didst give the law In cloud and majesty and awe.

O come, Thou Rod of Jessu, free Thine own from Satan's tyranny;

From depths of hell Thy people save, And give them victory o'er the grave.

O come, Thou Day-spring, come and cheer Our spirits by Thine advent here;
Disperse the gloomy clouds of night And death's dark shadows put to flight.

O come, Thou Key of David, come, And open wide our heavenly home;
Make safe the way that leads on high, And close the path to misery.

The present-day familiar stanzas included in this hymn, beginning "O come, Thou Wisdom from on high" and "O come, Desire of nations, come" were added later to complete the "Seven O's" by Dr. Henry Sloan Coffin, who is known to American Churchmen as the onetime President of New York City's Union Theological Seminary, and the prolific writer of a number of religious publications.

Appearing in one of Neale's collections for the first time in 1861, five years prior to his early death at the age of forty-eight, this carol began its ministry of song, enriching Christmas celebrations wherever it appeared. In no way as jubilant as some of the tunes to which children and young people used to dance during the Advent season, nor as sentimental as many of the perennial favorites of our own day that are resurrected with monotonous regularity every December, "O Come, O Come, Immanuel," with its dignity and restraint, its majesty and stateliness, continues to add its poignant musical ministry to the true spirit of the season, bringing with it a tie that extends back beyond the Middle Ages, reminding believers of every age that the news of the birth of the Son of God is always an occasion for merriment and mirth, and will always inspire rejoicing and singing until we see Him face to face.

Despite the rather pessimistic atmosphere in which he was compelled to perform most of his scholarly research, Neale's hymn breathes, even in the minor strains of the melody, a spirit of optimistic hopefulness that should always permeate everything associated with a Christmas celebration. As the poinsettia is sometimes considered not only a Christmas but also an Easter decoration, it is significant that the flowering genius of John Mason Neale gave us not only the beautiful Christmas hymns "O Come, O Come, Immanuel" and "Good Christian Men, Rejoice" but also the thrilling Easter hymns, "The Day Of Resurrection" and "Come Ye Faithful, Raise The Strain," and is remembered for his remarkable contributions to both of these most important festivals of the Christian calendar year. Such was the true spirit of the man that his epitaph, written by the preacher-poet himself some time before his death, contained this simple but revealing sentence: "J. M. Neale, poor and unworthy priest, resting under the sign of the Cross."

IN THE BLEAK MID-WINTER

All of the four children of Gabriele Rossetti, an Italian political refugee who fled from his native land to London and made his home there for many years, were unusually talented. Dante Gabriel won laurels both as a poet and as a painter; another son, William Michael, was a widely read critic; the eldest daughter, Maria Francesca, brought further fame to the family as a gifted writer, but it was the fourth child, and youngest of them all, Christina Georgina (1830-1894) whose poems eventually found their way into the Hymnals and Anthologies of the twentieth century.

Her brother Dante, two years her senior, and two fellow-painters, Holman Hunt and John E. Millais (not to be confused with the painter Millet of "The Angelus" and "The Man With The Hoe" fame) included Christina in their close intimate fellowship when they organized what they called The Pre-Raphaelite Brotherhood in 1848, the poet's eighteenth year, because she had already written some acceptable verses and given evidence of developing into a charming, beautiful and brilliant young woman. The influence of other artistic exiles who often crowded their London home inspired Christina to try her hand at writing original verses, even though the only formal training she had received in preparing for a poet's life had been at the hands of her father and mother. Her first efforts were welcomed so enthusiastically by her grandfather that he actually had them privately printed at his own expense, an indulgence he granted Dante two years later when he put up the money for the printing of one of the young lad's original stories. Mutual encouragement led both the brother and sister to continue writing until they had mastered the techniques of the craft, only to turn their talents then to other areas of artistic expression, in which one of them was eventually to excel.

The advice and counsel of another painter, Ford Madox Ford, brought the young painters and poets together in a fellowship dedicated to recapturing what they called "artistic freedom" by abandoning the classicism of the day and returning to the "pure art" as it had existed in the days before the great Italian painter, Raphael (1483-1520) gave the world his beautiful "Sistine Madonna," "The Madonna of the Chair" and other immortal masterpieces. Consequently they called themselves The Pre-Raphaelites. One result of their rebellion against what they considered "mediocrity and imitativeness" in current circles was Holman Hunt's greatest painting, "The Light Of The World," and Dante Rossetti's finest poem, "The Blessed Damozel," in both of which one finds "attention to detail, honesty, delicacy and sincerity" which were just what the idealistic young people wanted to convey by means of their brushes and pens.

Christina, who was born in London, December 5, 1830, possessed such "a religious beauty of face" as she grew into young womanhood that the members of the brotherhood used her as a model for many of their finest paintings, showing her not only as she actually was but also as they imagined her to be, surrounded by a mystical aura of other-worldly loveliness that seemed almost saintlike in its appearance.

While the youngest of the four Rossetti children was still

"a lively, precocious and clever" girl, she perfected her command and mastery of words and her gift of making beautiful rhymes so that her finest works revealed a childlike simplicity undergirded with a profound sincerity and stalwart Christian faith. Dante, meanwhile, was painting and poetizing in "overluxuriant colors" rich in imagery and permeated with mysticism. Christina's rare beauty of face and character attracted many men to her side, while her charming and disarming innocence merely served as an irresistible magnet that kept them hovering nearby, but almost always at an arm's length.

Because she was capable of loving deeply, she was soon a candidate for the sisterhood of the broken-hearted, for one man she loved was a Roman Catholic, whose offer of marriage she felt she had to decline, so intense was her personal devotion to the Anglican Church in which she herself held her membership, and to which faith she had given her complete devotion. That religious differences should come between a lover and her beloved never caused her own religious faith to falter, but only led her to seek God more intimately than ever before. Her poems reveal her inner struggle to reconcile these differences, and provide convincing proof that "love for God alone can keep the soul from going blind" in such hours of adversity and desperate loneliness. In her poem entitled "Twice" she wrote of taking her heart in her hand and presenting it to her lover, only to have him break it in two as he set it down, after which she had only a broken heart to offer to her God, with the prayer that He would "refine with fire its gold, Purge Thou its dross away—Yea, hold it in Thy hold, Whence none shall pluck it out," concluding with some lines that were later to be recast as the conclusion for her finest Christmas poem:

> I take my heart in my hand, I shall not die but live,
> Before Thy face I stand; I, for Thou callest such;
> All that I have I bring, All that I am I give,
> Smile Thou and I shall sing, But shall not question much.

Shattered youthful romances oftentimes led the poet to a morbid pre-occupation with death, a state that rarely escaped the sensitive soul of Christina Rossetti, despite her virile faith and the ever-beckoning promises of a brighter future. While, in one poem, she spoke of her "Birthday" as the day "when my love is come to me," she soon sank into such depths of despair that she wrote of dying, counselling her latest beloved to remember her and forget her all at the same time when she had gone away, only to conclude with this admonition, "Better by far you should forget and smile Than that you should remember and be sad." And, as if one could ever fully recover from such an experience, she told her dearest to "sing no sad songs" for her after her passing, but "if thou wilt, remember, And if thou wilt, forget," while, as for herself, she would hardly know the difference, for, resigning herself to her fate, she said, "Haply I may remember, And haply may forget." So she, who felt herself "contemned of a man" and "marred one heedless day" spurned every other proposal of marriage, and, toward the close of her life, gradually withdrew from the world, becoming "almost nunlike" in her avoidance of personal contacts with other people, and in the "aloofness" which characterized her dealings with the friends she formerly held so dear. The clarity of her mind, however, and the lucidity of her soul are perfectly mirrored in her children's poem:

> Who has seen the wind? Neither you nor I;
> But when the trees bow down their heads, The wind is passing by.

While her favorite brother Dante was bemoaning the loss of his beautiful wife, Elizabeth Siddal, after only two brief years of married bliss, Christina was trying to mend her own broken heart by sharing her miseries and burdens with him. When he actually buried an unpublished manuscript of his best poems in Elizabeth's casket, Christina felt he had not been true either to their great love or to his own developing talent. Several years later, having repented of his impulsive folly, Dante unearthed his deceased wife's coffin to retrieve his buried writings, an act that preserved for posterity some of his most inspired works, but which was severely criticized by some of his caustic critics as "an act of desecration" unworthy of such a brilliant artist and writer.

Christina's talent for painting a vivid picture with only a few words is never more clearly seen than in one of her briefest poems, a little Christmas gem of only three four-line verses which was published in the 1885 edition of her book, "Time Flies; A Reading Diary," in which she wrote:

Love came down at Christmas, Love all lovely, Love divine;
Love was born at Christmas, Stars and angels gave the sign.

Worship we the Godhead, Love incarnate, Love divine;
Worship we our Jesus; But wherewith for sacred sign?

Love shall be our token, Love be yours and love be mine,
Love to God and all men, Love for plea and gift and sign.

Her simple lines, like the remarkable strokes of the brush of a Japanese painter, say all that one feels is necessary to be said, while even the repetition of her theme is no more monotonous than that found in a Mozart sonata or minuet. When this tiny poem "where so much is said in so little space" was wedded later to the lilting Irish melody entitled "Garton," a favorite from County Donegal in the Ould Sod, a unique and delightful new Christmas carol was born.

In the columns of the Pre-Raphaelite publication, hopefully named "The Germ," many of Christina's and Dante's poems appeared in print for the first time, only to be included later in separate collections of their published and unpublished works. The disappointments of what she called "her earthly loves," instead of disillusioning her with all things sacred and holy, only drove her to intensify the quality and depth of her spiritual devotion and give herself more earnestly to the service of God as she knew Him in the person of His Son, Jesus Christ. It was in that spirit that, sometime before 1872, when the holiness of her beauty was maturing into the beauty of holiness with the passing of the years, she penned a descriptive poem of unusual charm dealing with the birth of Jesus, writing in a poetic meter so irregular that she felt it would never be the subject of a song or hymn, in precise and picturesque though sometimes repetitious phrases that said all that could be said poetically on the topic, yet concluding with an act of dedication reminiscent of earlier days and other poems, but unsurpassed in all Christmas literature, since it could be simultaneously lisped by a tiny child, spoken by an idealistic youth or whispered by an aged saint:

In the bleak mid-winter, Frosty wind made moan;
Earth stood hard as iron, Water like a stone;
Snow had fallen, snow on snow, Snow on snow,
In the bleak mid-winter, Long ago.

Our God, heaven cannot hold Him, Nor earth sustain;
Heaven and earth shall flee away, When He comes to reign;
In the bleak mid-winter, A stable-place sufficed
The Lord God Almighty, Jesus Christ.

Enough for Him Whom cherubim Worship night and day,
A breastful of milk And a mangerful of hay;
Enough for Him Whom angels Fall down before,
The ox and ass and camel Which adore.

Angels and archangels May have gathered there,
Cherubim and seraphim Thronged the air;
But His mother only, In her maiden bliss,
Worshipped the Beloved With a kiss.

What can I give Him, Poor as I am?
If I were a shepherd, I would bring a lamb;
If I were a wise man, I would do my part;
Yet what I can I give Him—Give my heart.

Her last two lines did not ask a question, "Yet what can I give Him?" but stated an affirmation, "Yet what I can I give Him," already demonstrated in the author's personal life.

When the British composer Gustav Holst set his hand to writing a suitable tune for these stanzas in 1906, two years after they had been published in a posthumous collection of Miss Rossetti's "Poetical Works," he adapted his music to the peculiarities of her several lines, naming the tune "Cranham" after Cranham Woods, a beauty spot not far from his birthplace near Cheltenham, England. The poet suffered a long and painful illness prior to her death on December 29, 1894, twenty-four days after her sixty-fourth birthday, having been born and having died in the month whose most dramatic

Christian festival had inspired two of her best and most enduring poems. The composer who made it possible for her stanzas to find their way into the Hymnals of the Church Universal also was the long-time victim of a serious, pain-wracking disease, but one would never dream that such a tune was born out of such privation and personal pain.

The Pre-Raphaelite Brotherhood died out when the charter members completed their life's work, but their influence is still being felt more than a hundred years after the inauguration of their fellowship, for Holman Hunt's painting, "The Light Of The World," which hangs in London's St. Paul's Cathedral, is a favorite the world over while Christina Rossetti's lovely Christmas hymns have become a part of the rich heritage which this generation is proud to bequeath to those to come.

MARY'S LULLABY

Sleep, baby Jesus,
  upon your bed of hay;
Mother will be watching
  until the break of day;
No oxen will be lowing,
  no little lamb will cry;
Sleep, baby Jesus,
  lullaby.

Sleep, baby Jesus,
  and close your tiny eyes;
Music of the angels
  is ringing through the skies.
You're such a helpless baby,
  I wonder, bye and bye;
Sleep, baby Jesus,
  lullaby.

Sleep, baby Jesus,
  the night is cold and still;
Shepherds watch are keeping
  out yonder on the hill.
A strange light fills the heavens,
  it may be God is nigh.
Sleep, baby Jesus,
  lullaby.

(This original Christmas carol has been a favorite of my Minister of Music brother, Henri Emurian, who has always had a soloist feature it one Sunday during December in every Church he has served as Director of Music and Organist.)

THE CHRISTMAS FLOWER

The Story of
THE POINSETTIA

THE CHRISTMAS FLOWER

Two South Carolinians had the rare privilege of having beautiful flowers named after them and in their honor, the first man being a practicing physician, Dr. Alexander Garden (1730-1791) and the second a professional politician, General Joel Roberts Poinsett (1779-1851). It was a Britisher who, in 1760, suggested that the Carolina doctor be so recognized while a native of Scotland made a similar suggestion with regard to the politician nearly three quarters of a century later, in 1836.

Dr. Alexander Garden was the second of three generations of Gardens who bore the same name, a fact which has caused much confusion among historians as they try to differentiate between the clergyman, who represented the first generation, the physician-botanist of the second generation and the military hero, politician and orator of the third generation, two of whom figured dramatically in the history of their country as well as their native state. The second generation Garden, the hero of this particular story, was born in Dirse Parish, Aberdeenshire, Scotland, the son of an honored clergyman, Rev. Dr. Alexander Garden (the First, or Senior, as the case may be). The director of the botanical gardens in Edinburgh introduced the medical student to the world of flowers, and, even though he took his Doctor of Medicine degree at Aberdeen's Marischal College in 1753, he was still a botanist at heart, and when he moved to South Carolina and began practicing medicine in Prince William Parish, he spent about as much time on his horticultural hobby as he devoted to medicine and the earning of a living, in both of which fields he proved himself well above the average. On December 24, 1755 he married Elizabeth Peronneau, and it was their son, who bore the traditional family surname, whom his father never forgave for siding with the Colonists during the War of American Independence. The good doctor himself never forgot his British heritage, sided openly with the British King during the war, arrogantly sent his personal congratulations to General Cornwallis after the Battle of Camden, and was consequently banished from his adopted state and sent back home to Great Britain after the final American victory and the cessation of hostilities, despite the fact that he was then a man of much wealth and culture, and had served his people in a variety of ways since moving to the new world. Although during a terrible smallpox epidemic in 1760 he had given of his time, talent and fortune to serve the dying and the distressed, nevertheless his property was confiscated in 1783, only to be restored again the following year. But Garden, ill of tuberculosis and dreading a recurrence of violent seasickness on a return voyage, remained in Europe the rest of his life, passing away in his Cecil Street home, London, still to the very end "a typical Georgia gentleman, refined, metaphysical, proud, touchy, choleric, often intolerant."

Garden had visited Greenville County, South Carolina in 1755, twenty-four years before Joel Poinsett's birth, studying its wildlife, cataloguing its mineral deposits and taking samples of its plant life. His report was regarded as worthy of publication, and, as one result of this printing, his creative endeavours and activities came to the attention of several leading British scientists. His correspondence with the English naturalist John Ellis, and the distinguished scientist who was considered the most learned man of the times in that field in the entire world, Linnaeus, carried his fame as a pioneer to distant lands and made it well-known among the botanists and naturalists of Britain and the continent. The fact that he held membership in the Royal Societies of London and Upsala is evidence of the esteem in which his discoveries were held by his fellow-scientists.

The climactic event of his life, and the one deed by which posterity remembers him, came when he discovered, cultivated and perfected a flower of the cape jasmine family, one originally native to tropical Asia and Africa. This particular flower on which Garden fastened his attention was one of a genus of over fifty species of shrubs, herbs and trees of the botanical family known as the Rubiacae. This special flower's symmetrical beauty and exotic fragrance were enhanced when the physician learned to pinch off all but a very few blossoms, particularly when several occurred at the leaf axil, and brought into existence what came to be regarded as a strikingly attractive discovery. It was his British correspondent, John Ellis, who, in 1760, suggested that the letters "i and a" be added to the doctor's name, thereby creating a new name "Gardenia" for the new flower. Those to whom he broached his suggestion accepted it enthusiastically, and Dr. Alexander Garden, for the thirty-one years prior to his death in 1791, had the satisfaction of knowing that he had not only brought forth a flower to beautify the world but also had been privileged to perpetuate his family name by means of its artistic excellence.

Twelve years before Dr. Garden died in London, Joel Roberts Poinsett was born in Charleston, South Carolina, March 2, 1779, the son of a leading physician of the city, Dr. Elisha P. Poinsett, and his wife Ann. After receiving his early education at the hands of his learned father and a local minister, Rev. J. H. Thompson, young Joel attended the Academy at Greenfield Hill, Connecticut, which was then administered by the Rev. Timothy Dwight, a clergyman later to gain well-merited fame as a president of Yale University and as the author of the well-known hymn "I Love Thy Kingdom, Lord." Following the completion of his studies under Dr. Dwight, young Poinsett crossed the Atlantic and matriculated in a Medical School in Edinburgh, Scotland, just nine years before Robert Buist, the man who was to play a prominent part in perpetuating Poinsett's name and influence, was born, not too far from the Scottish educational center. In addition to mastering medicine, Joel studied military science, learned several modern languages, and decided that a soldier's life was the life for him. Unfortunately his father did not concur with the young man's choice, and ordered Joel home and suggested, in no uncertain terms, that he take up the serious study of law. This being the furtherest thing from Joel's mind, this time the son refused to concur, and spent the next few years travelling around the world, finally returning home after an absence of seven years to bury his father and his sister, the last members of his own immediate family. While abroad, his personal contacts with such men as Napoleon, Alexander I and Metternich had whetted his appetite for military experience, but, the United States being nominally at peace, he found no field for the exercise of his acquired skills or for the application of many European theories of the science of war.

President James Madison, however, recognized the young man's innate abilities, and suggested him for Quartermaster General of the United States Army. The Secretary of War objected so violently that the President was persuaded to withdraw young Poinsett's name, and, instead, to save face as well as broaden his experience, sent him to South America as his personal agent to look after this country's interests during the threatened conflict that was due to break out any day between the United States and Great Britain. While Poinsett would have preferred an appointment in the field when the War of 1812 broke out, he was too far from home to be of any military value to his country so he spent two of those years in Chile, hatching out plots and counterplots for the benefit of his beloved homeland. When an insurrection in which he had played too open a part was exposed and crushed, there was nothing for the inexperienced politician to do but bid farewell to the Carrera brothers, with whom he had been collaborating in the abortive effort, and head for home. This he did, returning to Charleston in 1815.

When President James Monroe suggested a further South American mission during his term as Chief Executive of the growing Republic, Poinsett graciously declined, preferring the local political arena to the intrigues of South American politics. After two terms in the state legislature, during which he sponsored many reforms and promoted numerous projects for the betterment of his constituents, he ran for the House of Representatives, and succeeded Charles Pinckney as a member of Congress. In his four years in Washington, he is reputed to have delivered four speeches on four different subjects, none of which marked him for further political glory, so when he was asked to serve as a special envoy to Mexico in August, 1822, he accepted, acting in that capacity for a period of six months. Two years later, as a result of his familiarity with Mexican and South American politics, he was offered the post as the first official United States minister to Mexico, a position that several more ambitious political leaders had already declined for a number of reasons, mainly personal.

The British, who had succeeded in hounding Poinsett out of Chile in 1815, now tried to block his activities and influence in Mexico in 1825. They even had some of their well-paid stooges accuse him of trying to introduce Freemasonry into predominantly Roman Catholic Mexico, a charge brought about when Poinsett, at the request of some Masons in that country, asked the Grand Lodge of New York to issue a charter for them. His enemies dubbed him "an intriguer and expansionist," and spread such malicious tales about his activities that the Mexican government, undoubtedly being pressured behind the scenes by British agents, asked the President of the United States to recall him and relieve him of his office. After a five year stay, Poinsett added his own personal plea to that of his adversaries, and finally left Mexico City in January 1830.

Three years after returning to his Greenville County, South Carolina, home, having moved there from Charleston in 1819, Poinsett married Mrs. Mary Pringle, the widow of a deceased friend, and settled down on his plantation to enjoy catching up on his reading as well as cultivating the flowers that grew in splendid profusion all around him. The fact that his enemies considered his mission to Mexico a failure did not faze him, and he went about his daily routine with a sense of satisfaction and personal devotion that the fortunes of a political arena can neither create nor destroy.

During his stay in Mexico, Poinsett had been fascinated by a new type of plant he saw growing there in its natural habitat, one he had never seen growing in the United States, and he quickly learned that the plant was actually a local species of Euphorbia, sometimes spoken of as a Lobster-flower, and at other times as a Mexican Flame-leaf or Fire-plant. He later discovered that it was more of a plant than a flower, and was "a tropical herb or shrubby plant belonging to the spurge family, whose gorgeous colored leaves were often mistaken for flowers," the colored leaves having been mistaken for petals. The two Mexican types were known technically as the fire-plant and the heterophylla, while the type generally handled by commercial florists today is known as the pulcherrima. The Mexican Minister was curious to know whether the strange and unusual plants would flourish as well in the climate of South Carolina as they did farther south in Mexico, so he had several of them shipped to his home, with strict instructions as to their care and handling. When Poinsett began the careful cultivation of the new flowers or plants during this period of semi-retirement from public affairs, the word began to spread that the General had discovered an entirely new flower, the like of which had never been seen in the United States before.

One of those who heard the rather startling news, together with a careful, accurate description of the strange discovery, was Robert Buist, the native of Scotland who had come to America and was at that time associated with a Mr. Hibbert in the floral business in Philadelphia. His curiosity was aroused and he carefully and closely examined the finest encyclopedias for some word about the new plant, only to find that the most authentic reference books were silent on the subject. Buist was no novice in the field, although at that time, in 1836, he was only thirty-one years of age. A native of Cupar Fyfe near Edinburgh, Scotland, where he was born on November 14, 1805, Robert early devoted himself to the practice of gardening, studying with the one-time curator of the Edinburgh Botanic Garden, Mr. James Mc-Nab. His interests being aroused, he furthered his training in the famous gardens of the Earl of Harrington at Elvaston Castle, generally reckoned one of the finest in the British Empire. It was natural that when Buist came to the United States in 1828 he sought out the head of the leading nursery in the country and asked for employment, so David Landreth, the outstanding man in this new but expanding profession, put him to work immediately. Later he became associated with Henry Pratt, whose gardens were as famous in the new world as were those of the Earl of Harrington in the old. When young Robert arrived in Philadelphia there were three leading nurseries in the city, Bartram's, Rising Sun, and Hibbert's, the last being the oldest of the three. In 1830, Buist became Mr. Hibbert's partner, and the store they opened at Twelfth and Lombard Streets did an enormous amount of business, assisted, no doubt, by the successful grand exhibition which the Pennsylvania Horticultural Society had sponsored the previous year. Both Hibbert and Buist gained enviable reputations for themselves by importing rare plants and flowers from all over the world, and it came as something of a shock and surprise to the young business man that he had no record whatsoever of a plant that in any remote manner resembled the one which he learned General Poinsett was cultivating on his South Carolina plantation. Consequently, there was nothing for him to do but to travel south and see this new horticultural wonder for himself, and decide whether the rumors that had been creeping north were fact or fiction. On the scene at last, Buist learned that the General had been quite successful in transplanting the Mexican fire-plant from its native shady and damp tropical climate to the soil and climate of his native state, and he marvelled all the more at the attractiveness as well as at the hardiness of the new discovery, urging Poinsett to let the Philadelphia firm of Hibbert and Buist be the sole distributors of the new plant throughout the United States. When the two men agreed to this business proposition, they found themselves unable to agree on a practical name for the new plant. Lobster-flower and fire-plant seemed too unrealistic, while flame-flower appeared to be somewhat too exotic. Then it was that the thirty-one year old Philadelphian suggested to the fifty-seven year old retired politician that they take a page right out of South Carolina's own noble history and do for Poinsett's new plant what Britisher John Ellis had suggested for Dr. Alexander Garden's new flower. While Poinsett naturally and modestly objected, Buist insisted, and when he returned to the City of Brotherly Love with several of the new plants in his proud possession, he told his partner and his employees that he had merely added the letters "i and a" to the name of the discoverer, General Poinsett, and named the new plant "poinsettia" (not "poinsetta" with the letter "i" omitted).

In his later years, as his knowledge and influence grew, Robert Buist wrote three books, "Rose Manual," 1847, "Flower Garden Directory," 1851, and "Family Kitchen Garden," 1851, as well as many articles for numerous periodicals. A tall, erect man who often was pointed out with pride as a typical Scotch Presbyterian, Mr. Buist was thrice married. When his eldest son passed away, his other son and namesake, Robert Buist, took over the family business, carrying it on in the traditions of his famous father after the elder Buist's death at Rosedale, Philadelphia, July 13, 1880. In addition to naming Poinsett's plant, Buist suggested new names for other botanical improvements and discoveries, his worth to his own city being recognized when a street in Philadelphia was named for him when the growing metropolis finally annexed the land which the Buist farms had formerly occupied. The Robert Buist Company, distributors of superior seeds, bought out the D. Landreth Company in 1946, an event which created much interest since Mr. Landreth, who established his firm in 1784 had given Robert Buist his first job when the young Scotchman arrived in the United States in 1828. The Landreth and Buist companies are now "the two oldest seed houses in America."

As for General Poinsett, he was soon summoned from his "retirement" by President Martin Van Buren who wanted him to fill the post of Secretary of War in his new Cabinet, a position the learned country gentleman accepted and occupied with distinction throughout Van Buren's administration. Among the accomplishments of his four-year tenure were these: the organization of a General Staff; advocation of Universal Military Training to defend the nation's distant frontiers; relocation of thousands of Indians to reservations beyond the Mississippi River and the termination of several Indian Wars within the boundaries of several of the states;

an enlarged course of study at West Point and a better equipped army with more modern weapons for the discharging of their duties to the country at large. Regarded in his more mature years as "a man of wide interests and broad scope of literary, scientific, philosophical, historical, botanical and philanthropic interests," Joel Roberts Poinsett authored one popular volume, "Notes on Mexico made in 1822, with an Historical Sketch of the Revolution," and was awarded an honorary L.L.D. degree by Columbia University in 1825. He was one of those rare Americans who turned down a proffered commission in the Russian Army, preferring to give his services to the welfare, betterment, peace and prosperity of the American people.

Once again, in 1841, he retired to his South Carolina plantation, this time for the last time, taking thereafter little activity in local or national politics, dying near Statesburg, Sumter County, on December 12, 1851 at the age of seventy-two, and being buried in the Cemetery of the Church of the Holy Cross in that village. While Poinsett's only claim to military fame rested upon one rather reckless act of daring during his stay in South America, when he successfully led a force of Chilean Republicans against some Spaniards and recaptured several American merchant ships which the Spaniards had seized during the War of 1812, he had the most unusual distinction of having given his name to a plant or flower that is presently regarded as both a Christmas and an Easter decoration. While the carols of the Advent and the Resurrection seasons are never interchangeable, and while an Easter lily would seem incongruous beneath a Christmas tree and out of place beside a traditional manger scene, nevertheless, the poinsettia seems to be at home at the celebration of both the Lord's birth and His resurrection. If Poinsett and Buist had collaborated on this one successful project alone, their long lives and many wanderings would have been eminently worthwhile.

DARK THE NIGHT, SO COLD AND LONELY

8.7.8.7.D.

Dark the night, so cold and lonely,
When the mighty Lord of all,
Came to earth, was born of Mary
In an empty cattle stall.
Shepherds knelt in adoration;
Hosts of angels sang above,
"Christ is born, of man the Saviour,
Prince of Peace and Lord of Love."

Far across the eastern mountains,
Bearing costly gifts and rare,
Came the wise men, longing, seeking
For a wondrous child and fair.
Overhead a star shone brightly,
Guiding to that sacred shrine,
Where the new-born son of Mary
Slept amidst the lowing kine.

Join we all the angel chorus,
Man has prayed and not in vain;
God hath sent His promised Saviour,
Christ is born in Bethlehem.
Hasten we to pay our homage,
To His feet our tribute bring;
Hail th' incarnate God of glory,
Christ the Lord and Christ the King.

The tune for this carol was composed several years before the words were written. It was only when I played the music for a friend who suggested that it would make a good Christmas hymn that I prepared these three stanzas. While my tune, named "Baboo," after the pet name we have called our Father ever since we were little children, is included in my booklet of original HYMNS, these stanzas may be sung to such familiar tunes as "Love Divine," "Ton-Y-Botel," "Autumn" or any other 8.7.8.7.D. hymn tune.

GOOD KING WENCESLAUS

The Story of
A CHRISTMAS CAROL

GOOD KING WENCESLAUS

The lives and influences of five different men in five different countries over a span of nearly nineteen centuries resulted in one of Christendom's most joyous Christmas carols. While the five stanzas of "Good King Wenceslaus" tell an interesting story of an unusual monarch, by no stretch of the imagination could they be considered a Christian hymn, since none of their lines are "addressed to or descriptive of one of the Persons in the Holy Trinity, the Father, the Son and the Holy Ghost." Nevertheless, hardly is December upon us than we begin to hear once again the perennially familiar lilting cadences of the tune "Tempus Adest Floridum" with which this narrative poem has become permanently wedded.

The first man to be considered in this brief account is not only the first chronologically but also the first in importance, since he is none other than the first Christian martyr, Stephen, whose story is told with dramatic intensity in the Book of Acts, chapters six through eight. This young Greek-speaking Jewish convert to the Christian faith was regarded as a believer of such marked ability that he was chosen one of the first seven "deacons" of the Church in Jerusalem, and charged with the responsibility of taking care of the business end of the growing fellowship, especially that part of it that had to do with the feeding of the needy widows from the common treasury. Not only did Stephen perform this rather perfunctory duty with diligence and dispatch, but he also began witnessing to his new-found faith by preaching alongside the eleven apostles themselves. The emotional fervor of his preaching coupled with the brilliance with which he confounded his critics in open discussion and debate soon marked him as a man to be reckoned with on the part of those who violently opposed the followers of The Way. It was not long before Stephen was summoned by the Sanhedrin, the highest Jewish Council that attempted to exercise authority over civil as well as over ecclesiastical affairs, and accused of speaking blasphemy against the Jewish law as well as treason against the Jewish faith and Church. These trumped-up charges, supported by well-paid false witnesses who testified against the accused, made a complete mockery of the supposed fair trial until Stephen took affairs in his own capable hands, and in a masterful address in his own defense accused his accusers of the very sins for which they were seeking judgment against him. Unable to reply to his unanswerable arguments, the members of the Council chose to silence him rather than offer a rebuttal to his well-founded charges against them, and, in a frenzy of unrighteous wrath gnashed on him with their teeth, dragged him outside the walls of the city so as not to violate a Jewish law against stoning a person to death within the confines of the holy city itself, and there pounded and pummelled him to death with rocks and stones. The young martyr, whose face had been "as the face of an angel" a short while before, now gazed into heaven and caught a glimpse of glory. Then, calling to his Master, he cried, "Lord Jesus, receive my spirit," but before expiring, remembering what he had heard about his Master's cruel crucifixion and recalling the first saying from the cross, he added, "Lord, lay not this sin to their charge," and then fell into the sleep of death.

His martyrdom was not in vain, however, for it resulted in the spiritual awakening and eventual conversion of an interested by-stander, Paul of Tarsus, and possibly preached a more eloquent sermon than any words the youth had uttered during his all too brief life of less than thirty-three years.

Significantly the name of this first Christian martyr was adapted from another Greek word "stephanos," which literally means "crown." While there are two Greek words that can be translated "crown," the first one, "diadema" refers merely to the actual crown or diadem which is the mark of royalty. It was this idea that inspired Edward Perronet to incorporate the phrase "Bring forth the royal diadem and crown Him Lord of all" in his hymn "All Hail The Power Of Jesus' Name." On the other hand, a "stephanos" is a crown that is used on three different occasions to signify three varied accomplishments: it is a crown of victory, presented in the form of a laurel wreath to the winner in an athletic contest; it is likewise regarded as a crown of festivity, generally worn by newlyweds during the wedding ceremony and subsequent merry-making; and it is also awarded as a crown of charity and service to well-deserving public servants as an act of appreciation for unselfish and faithful devotion to "the common welfare of all the citizens." The life and death of Stephen certainly exemplified victory, festivity and charity, and it was later deemed unusually appropriate that the first Christian martyr bore such a fitting name.

Soon after the twenty-fifth of December was agreed upon as a suitable date for the celebration of the birthday of Jesus, since by that time the winter solstice has passed and the days once again begin to encroach upon the nights, the light gradually overcoming the darkness, symbolic of Him whom God sent as the Light of the world to overcome the darkness of sin and death, the Christians of the fourth century began to participate in another celebration the very next day, December twenty-sixth, setting that day aside as St. Stephen's Day, in honor of the first martyr to give his life for his Lord. This practice spread from Jerusalem to the near corners of Christendom, and when the body of the sainted martyr was said to have been discovered somewhere in Palestine about the year 415 A.D. further interest in his life and death caused the custom to become even more widespread. In the latter half of the fifth century, Pope Simplicius, who ruled as the Supreme Pontiff of the Roman Catholic Church from 468 until 483, dedicated a Church on Rome's Coelian Hill to St. Stephen, who by that time had already been canonized by the Church, and it was considered quite suitable that "the first among saints, after the festival of the Lord's nativity, should be the one who first gave his life for his faith in his Redeemer." It was in honor of this martyr that Bishop Reginald Heber (1783-1826) later wrote his St. Stephen's

Day hymn, "The Son Of God Goes Forth To War" in which he described Stephen's death in the second stanza:

That martyr first, whose eagle eye Could pierce beyond the grave,
Who saw his Master in the sky And called on Him to save;
Like Him, with pardon on his tongue In midst of mortal pain,
He prayed for them that did the wrong; Who follows in his train?

While many monarchs ruled many countries during the first nine centuries of the Christian era and were revered as good men and honored for the piety of their lives as well as the purity of their faith, it was not until the tenth century that a ruler appeared upon the European scene who was holy enough in personal life and official administration to become famed in song and story as "Good King Wenceslaus." Generally there seems to have been, during the centuries of recorded history, more bad kings than good ones, although in the Biblical account of the birth of Jesus there was just one evil king, who bore the name Herod, while there were three good kings, the rulers, wise men or Magi who came from out of the east to visit the young child and lay their gifts in homage at his little feet. While good kings may have outnumbered bad kings three to one ever since, the bad ones seem, in many instances, to get better publicity, either because their badness is considered more notorious and therefore more newsworthy, or else because these bad kings had sense enough to hire more efficient public relations men on their staffs. Anyway, the first of five rulers to bear the name of Wenceslaus was good enough to be revered and remembered as such, even though his earthly life was about as brief as that of St. Stephen, and despite the fact that he, too, suffered a martyr's death for his Christian faith.

The future Duke, Prince or King Wenceslaus of Bohemia was born in 903 A.D., the son of a pious Christian ruler, Duke Wratislaw, and his pagan wife, Dragomir. Bohemia, one of those central European kingdoms that traced its history back to pre-Christian times, more than likely took its name from the tribes known as the Boii who inhabited and occupied the territory during the days of the Roman empire. When Christian missionaries attempted to bring the new faith to the Bohemian people from Germany in the west, the natives rejected it in no uncertain terms because of their deep-seated distrust of everything Germanic. Later, when other preachers came from Moravia in the east, they found a warmer welcome and were granted a more receptive hearing, as a result of which the Bohemian prince Borivoj was baptized as a Christian in the year 873 by a saintly priest named Methodius (825-885) and his subjects rapidly accepted the new faith.

Methodius, known affectionately as The Apostle to the Slavs, had gone to Moravia with his younger brother Constantine, who adopted the name Cyril, in the year 863 at the invitation of King Ratislav, going from there to adjacent Bohemia ten years later. The Greek Church canonized the two brothers, setting aside February 14 as St. Cyril's Day and May 11 as St. Methodius' Day. The Roman branch of divided Catholicism set aside March 9 as their joint feast day following their canonization by Pope Leo XIII in 1881.

When Duke Wratislaw died, his widow was so outspokenly hostile to the Christian faith, in spite of the fact that her subjects had embraced the new religion voluntarily and were in no mood to revert to their former pagan practices, that the twenty-five year old prince was urged to seize control of the government and supplant his mother as the people's ruler. As he had been reared principally by his pious grandmother Ludmilla, Wenceslaus (whose name in German is also Wenzel) did just that. Because she instructed the lad in the tenets of Christianity, Ludmilla incurred the enmity of her daughter-in-law, Dragomir, and it was at the command of the younger woman that the older one was strangled to death by hired assassins at Tetin on September 16, 921.

While Wenceslaus should have been able to read "the handwriting on the wall" when notified of that treacherous deed, he refused to believe that his mother could be capable of such cruelty. To stem the tide of this pagan reaction, the young king ruled with a firmness coupled with patience, trying to overlook and forgive the evil designs of the worst of his sworn enemies, but with Christian forbearance and charity always looking for the best in everyone. His acts of kindness soon became legendary throughout his kingdom, even though his rule was a brief one, and the story of his willingness to go out on a bitter cold night "on the Feast Day of St. Stephen," the day after Christmas, to feed a starving subject was entirely consistent with the manner of life he lived during his years as Duke, Prince or King of Bohemia.

Wenceslaus even took the vow of celibacy, and devoted himself with Christian abandon to the service of his people. Because of his many virtues he became known before his tragic and untimely death at the age of thirty-two as "Wenceslaus the Holy." Incensed at his growing Christian influence and determined to crush the new faith once and for all, his mother Dragomir, who had plotted the death of St. Ludmilla, now schemed to destroy her own son, in spite of the fact that Emperor Otto I had conferred upon him all the titles and dignity of his exalted office. Conspiring with Wenceslaus' younger brother Boleslav, and promising to put him on the throne once his older brother was out of the way, she goaded her second son until he took a sharp hatchet in his hand and personally hacked his saintly brother to death at the door of his own Church of Alt-Bunzlau on September 28, 935.

After Boleslav ascended the throne, the memory of his fratricidal deed haunted him to such an extent that he felt compelled to do penance for his dastardly crime. Three years after slaying his brother, the new king repented, and had Wenceslaus' remains reburied in the Church of St. Vitus in Prague. The gathering of his relics was thereafter celebrated on June 27, his translation on March 4 and the date of his martyrdom, September 28, set aside as his feast day.

In the hearts of his faithful followers, Stephen and Wenceslaus the Holy were esteemed as brother martyrs for the cause of Christ, and the fact that their King had performed many of his charitable deeds on December 26, St. Stephen's Day, became the subject and theme of many a spontaneous lyric while his unselfish acts of liberality began to be immortalized by troubadours and wandering minstrels as they sang of his goodness and lauded the saintly purity and singular beauty of his life in the songs they sang in castle and palace during their meanderings through central Europe. As the dark ages descended upon that section of the world, and as one by one the lights of faith and culture were extinguished when barbarian hordes over-ran the country and destroyed what had once been a flourishing Christian civilization, the memories of Good King Wenceslaus' noble character and faithful obedience to his Lord stood out in bolder relief, while the qualities he inculcated in his own life were regarded as more Christlike with the passing of time.

In order to keep the historical record straight, there were four more rulers who bore the same name, none of whom achieved in his personal life the qualities of saintliness which belong to Wenceslaus the Holy (903-935) alone. In a class all by himself, he was given not a Number but a Name. Wenceslaus I, the son of Ottokar I, ruled as king during the years 1230-1253, being succeeded to the throne by his son Ottokar II, who was in turn followed by Wenceslaus II, a grandson of Wenceslaus I. He served under a regent from 1278 until 1283, ruling in his own right thereafter until his death in 1305. His son, Wenceslaus III (1289-1306) was King of Hungary from 1301 until 1304 and King of Bohemia the last two years of his life, 1305 and 1306. Wenceslaus IV, the last and most notable of the line, the son of Charles IV of Holy Roman Empire fame, was King of Germany and of the Holy Roman Empire from 1378 until 1400, ruling over Bohemia alone from that date until his death in 1419. This was the Wenceslaus who ruled during the life, ministry, arrest, trial and martyrdom of the Bohemian "morning-star of the Reformation" John Huss. But of them all, only Wenceslaus the Holy, the patron saint of his native land, was later canonized by the Roman Catholic Church and officially given a feast day, September 28. Like St. Stephen, he earned the right to wear the "stephanos," the triple tiara of victory, festivity and charity, the true crown of genuine Christians. While the legends linking the King with the first martyr's feast day continued to be told and retold, the tunes to which their poetic versions were being sung were gradually forgotten. As the stories began to be recast in other languages, old phrases and melodies were soon disregarded as just so much chaff, until the kernel of truth alone survived the passing of the centuries. When, during the middle of the sixteenth century, a young student from Finland became interested in collecting some popular melodies of his day in order to make them available for his own people, he had no idea that he was unwittingly paving the way for the eventual preservation of the legend of Good King Wenceslaus in poetic form. For Didrik Pederson (whose name has been variously rendered in different languages as Theodoricus Petrus and Theodoric Petri) was more concerned with gathering together an authentic collection of familiar folk-tunes of his day than he was with perpetuating a story about a kindly king who had lived and reigned five centuries earlier in a land far removed from his own.

The youth from Abo undertook this project while studying at the University of Rostock, and one of the pieces of music he considered worthy of being included in his proposed publication was a Scandinavian melody arranged for a Latin poem that, being translated, began "Spring Has Now Unwrapped The Flowers." Under the Latin name "Tempus Adest Floridum," the Finnish compiler added this selection to his new volume. It was somewhat different from most of the other tunes, however, since many of them were written in the plainsong style of the thirteenth and fourteenth centuries, flowing along in the free manner of those ancient melodies, and therefore difficult to adapt to more modern poetic meters. "Tempus Adest Floridum," though, was readily adaptable to a good poem written in the meter known popularly as 7.6.7.6.D. provided the accent was placed on the first syllable of each line and not on the second as most 7.6.7.6.D. poems did. For example, the tunes "Webb" (Stand Up, Stand Up For Jesus), "Aurelia" (The Church's One Foundation) and "Lancashire" (Lead On, O King Eternal) are composed for poems written with seven syllables in the first, third, fifth and seventh lines and six syllables in the second, fourth, sixth and eighth lines. But in reading, reciting or singing these hymns, one does not accent the first and third syllables, but the second and the fourth in this manner, "Stand UP, stand UP for JEsus," or "Lead ON, o KING eTERnal." But the tune Pederson liked was adaptable only to a 7.6.7.6.D. (the D meaning you double the four-line poem and make it an eight-line poem) poem that accented the first syllable of the poem and subsequently accented the third, fifth and seventh syllables of the first line rather than the second, fourth and sixth, as in "TEMpus ADest FLOriDUM" or "SPRING has NOW unWRAPPED the FLOWERS," which would be rather awkward if not entirely impossible to sing if forced into the usual 7.6.7.6.D. pattern, with the accent on the other syllables instead.

This supposedly traditional Swedish tune and others known today as "Divinum Mysterium" and "Puer Nobis Nascitur" were published in 1582 in the author's volume entitled "Piae Cantiones," a collection that proved tremendously popular, although the editor little dreamed that nearly three-hundred years later a British Anglican divine would take the joyous music of his "springtime carol" and make it world renowned as the tune for a new "Christmas carol." Many of the "exquisite tunes" from this sixteenth century publication were picked up by the Reformed Lutherans of Finland and Sweden and, with sacred stanzas adapted to their peculiarities of meter, were used in services of public worship throughout the two countries.

During the middle of the nineteenth century, when the new British Minister to Sweden providentially came upon a copy of "Piae Cantiones" in the National Museum in Stockholm, he was keen enough to recognize a remarkable discovery when he accidentally stumbled upon one, and quickly conveyed the good news of what he had had the good fortune to find to a fellow-Britisher back home in England, Rev. John Mason Neale (1818-1866), the remarkable Anglican clergyman whose original hymns, translations of ancient and medieval Greek and Latin hymns and other scholarly accomplishments have placed all Christendom in his debt. Had Neale done no more than write such original hymns, inspired by ancient texts, as the Christmas favorite, "Good Christian Men, Rejoice," from the old Latin free-verse poem "In Dulci Jubilo," and the conversational question and answer hymn, "Art Thou Weary, Art Thou Languid?", and translated such masterpieces of thought, construction and expression as the Palm Sunday gem, "All Glory, Laud And Honor," the Easter hymns, "Come Ye Faithful, Raise The Strain" and "The Day Of Resurrection," and the surpassingly beautiful hymn on heaven, "Jerusalem The Golden," as well as the vigorous, "Christian, Dost Thou See Them?", his forty-eight years would not merely have been well spent, they would have been wisely invested. But he not only wrote and translated such outstanding works as the aforementioned sacred hymns, he also penned biographies, essays on Church history and hymns and sacred poems on a wide variety of related subjects for all ages, children, youth and adults, while eking out an existence as warden of an endowed Church-supported almshouse known as Sackville College, at East Grinstead, some twenty-five miles south of London, England, at a salary that would be considered only a little more than a pittance. The richest and most productive twenty years of his life were spent looking after the aged and indigent who were sent to Sackville because there was no other place to which they could go.

While Neale suffered from ill-health and was prevented thereby from accepting one or two more lucrative appointments in the Church of England, nevertheless "he was treated most unjustly by his ecclesiastical superiors" who never caught a glimpse of the genius hiding behind the preacher-poet's polite and gracious exterior. In spite of the haughty attitudes of those who shunted him aside when better preferments were available, Neale settled down to take care of the aged, the orphans and the unwed mothers who came to him begging for help, meantime digging up the glories of bygone centuries and making them available for his own Church in his own tongue for his own and subsequent generations. When his own Alma Mater, Cambridge University, failed to recognize him as an illustrious son and confer upon him an honorary degree in keeping with Neale's personal accomplishments, Harvard University in the United States saw to it that he became the recipient of an honorary Doctor of Divinity degree, one of the few such awards that honored both the donor and the receiver alike.

When Neale heard from the British Minister in Stockholm, he asked that a copy of the three century old book be made available to him for his private study and use. His request was granted, and a copy of "Piae Cantiones" is now in the safe keeping of the British Museum.

When he glanced through its yellowed pages, Neale quickly marked several tunes as worthy of further consideration. He had just been perfecting a rather unusual new poem that could hardly be called a hymn or even a sacred song, prior to being notified of the Stockholm discovery, and he considered it almost an act of providence that the stanzas he had but recently completed in 7.6.7.6.D. poetic meter needed just such a tune as he had suddenly come across in Pederson's volume of three-hundred years ago. Neale, preparing a new collection to be entitled "Carols for Christmastide," scheduled for publication in 1853, had versified the legend of King Wenceslaus the Holy in the form of a conversation between the King and one of his pages, writing five stanzas before completing the narrative in poetic form to his own satisfaction, and the lilting strains of Tune Number Fifty-Two in the Swedish publication, a tune named "Tempus Adest Floridum," seemed made to order for the new carol, for Neale had expressed himself in this manner:

Good King Wenceslaus looked out On the Feast of Stephen,
When the snow lay round about, Deep and crisp and even;
Brightly shone the moon that night, Though the frost was cruel,
When a poor man came in sight, Gathering winter fuel.

"Hither, page, and stand by me, If thou know'st it, telling;
Yonder peasant, who is he? Where and what his dwelling?"
"Sire, he lives a good league hence, Underneath the mountain;
Right against the forest fence, By Saint Agnes' fountain."

"Bring me flesh and bring me wine, Bring me pinelogs hither;
Thou and I will see him dine When we bear them thither."
Page and monarch forth they went, Forth they went together;
Through the rude wind's wild lament, And the bitter weather.

"Sire, the night is darker now, And the wind blows stronger;
Fails my heart, I know not how, I can go no longer."
"Mark my footsteps, my good page, Tread thou in them boldly;
Thou shalt find the winter's rage Freeze thy blood less coldly."

In his master's steps he trod, Where the snow lay dinted;
Heat was in the very sod Which the saint had printed;
Therefore, Christian men, be sure, Wealth or rank possessing,
Ye who now will bless the poor, Shall yourselves find blessing.

At the suggestion of a friend and co-worker, Rev. Thomas Helmore, Neale took the joyous tune for the springtime carol which Pederson had included in his publication and incorporated it as a new tune for his Christmas carol "Good King Wenceslaus," publishing them in the 1853 collection, "Carols For Christmastide." The carol became so rapidly popular that many people regarded it as an ancient English folksong recently revived, and found it hard to believe that it had come from the pen of the erudite scholar and superb hymn-writer, John Mason Neale. While the author knew he was not writing a hymn, he was conscious of the fact that his carol could play a prominent role all its very own with the coming of each Advent season, a conviction which the passing of time has authenticated in a convincing manner. While the tune has been harmonized variously by such musical giants as Sir John Stainer and Sir Ernest Campbell MacMillan, the melody and mood remain exactly as they were when Pederson first printed them and the British Minister discovered them and Neale adapted them to his own peculiar poetic needs. In an attempt to make the tune available for regular Church services, a British clergyman who spent most of his active years preaching in Canada, Rev. Joseph Simpson Cook (1859-1933), wrote his new carol, "Gentle Mary Laid Her Child, Lowly In A Manger," first published in a Canadian Church Hymnal in 1930. While the carol is gradually gaining favor, those who sing it invariably say, "Why, that's the tune for 'Good King Wenceslaus,' " which is proof enough that it will be a long, long time before Neale's poem is forgotten, if ever!

ANGELS IN THE SNOW

How I remember
Long ago December,
Happy children making angels in the snow;
While we were sleighing
We would see them playing,
Happy children making angels in the snow.
Christmas chimes were ringing,
Heavenly choirs were singing,
Santa's toys were bringing
Joy to every heart.
How I remember
Long ago December,
Happy children making angels in the snow.

(Words and Music Copyright 1957, E. K. E.)

In some of the northern states when the snow is too dry to pack into snowballs or fashion into snowmen, the children have a delightful custom of making Angels In The Snow. They lie down on the dry snow and wave their outstretched arms back and forth, leaving, when they rise, what resembles the figure of a winged angel in the snow. It was a painting of just such a scene on the cover of a December issue of The Saturday Evening Post some years ago that inspired me to write this little Christmas song.

THE STORY OF A CHRISTMAS POEM

'Twas the Night Before Christmas

'TWAS THE NIGHT BEFORE CHRISTMAS

The origins of some of our present day Christmas customs are lost in the mists of antiquity, but others can be traced to definite traditions in different countries while still others have been romanticized beyond their relative importance with the passing of time, or given a halo of holiness they never possessed in the past. The ancient custom of bringing in the Yule Log was not the sentimental act that some modern authors have pictured it to be nor was it the semi-religious ceremony that others have portrayed. The fact is that some of our ancestors were fun-loving, work-shirking, half-lazy ne'er-do-wells, who sat around and drank too much of their particular national beverage, since Europeans never drink water because of its impurities or because they can't stand its "neutral" taste, while their wives and children did all the work. In the winter time, the women folk by means of black coffee and wifely nagging managed to get these trifling males out of the house and into the woods long enough each day to chop down a small sapling and cut up enough firewood to last through the day and night, repeating the process with monotonous regularity day after day throughout every long, cold and hard winter. Having little foresight, these ancient sires never thought of cutting up enough wood for more than one day at a time. Yet when Christmas came around every December, they regarded it merely as a good excuse to double up on their drinking, with the result that their families generally froze their way through the holiday season. Consequently a few of the more energetic women promised their red-nosed spouses that they could imbibe as freely as they wanted to during the holidays provided they brought enough wood into the house to fill the fireplace with a roaring fire while they were enjoying their binges and getting over the effects of their over-indulgence. The men reluctantly consented and got together to drag logs into each other's cabin or hut, so they could drink together in undisturbed peace the rest of the season. No wonder then that the bringing in of what they called The Christmas Log or the Yule Log was an occasion for a celebration! It was the only time during the winter that the wife was assured of a good fire for more than one day at a time. All this hullabaloo about the practice being derived from tree-worship on the part of ancient tribes and all the sentimental slush about young boys vying for the glorious privilege of having a hand in dragging in the Yule Log "ain't necessarily so." The only element of truth in the story consists in the fact that this was the only time throughout the entire winter that a large log was brought into the house and placed in the fireplace to provide heat, warmth and light for the family while the husband and father was out somewhere drinking his "Christmas cheer" or lying around on the floor sleeping off the effects of a previous pre-holiday celebration!

As for the feudal serf whose Lord refused to permit him to cut down any trees for any purpose whatsoever, the gift of a log at Christmas time was regarded as a generous act on the part of the gracious Master, but even at that it was the only time during the entire year that the Lord of the manor granted his serfs that favor, and its arrival was greeted with the same enthusiam for the very same reason.

When a man looked out of his living room window one Christmas eve and saw a group of men in the act of bringing in a large object through the front door of the house next door, he said to a companion nearby, "Well, what do you know? There's my neighbor Murphy bringing in the Yule Log." His friend took a cursory glance at the situation and remarked rather coldly, "Oh, it's nothing of the sort. It's some of his friends bringing in Murphy!"

As for the use of gold, frankincense and myrrh in remembrance of the gifts that the Magi brought to the infant Jesus when they made their long trek from the east even unto Bethlehem, the first present of gold is still a valued commodity to this very day, while the third gift, myrrh, is still associated with the burial of the dead and the embalmer's art in most oriental lands. It is the second present, frankincense, that puzzles people, and to satisfy their curiosity we are told that incense was always burned in the presence of a King, the more important the monarch the more expensive the incense. The truth of the matter is that frankincense was nothing more than very expensive old-timy "Air Wick," which was used to counteract or cover up or neutralize the awful smells that permeated most castles in those early days. With the cattle and sheep sleeping in the courtyard and with no bath-tubs for the regular washing of the human body, those places actually smelled to high heaven! So when royal personages came by, costly incense was burned to kill off the horrible odors and make the place fit for human habitation. Today, with our modern standards of cleanliness, we have little use for the burning of incense save as a pagan carry-over in some religious circles and for personal reasons of a rather romantic nature.

Since the Wise Men came from the east, and since poor Christians had neither gold nor frankincense nor myrrh, they gathered up some spices that came from the orient lands, baked them in some dough, called the concoction a "mince-meat pie," when it was neither mince nor meat nor pie, and thereby remembered the Three Kings when they ate their humble Christmas dinners in their poverty-stricken homes.

As far as the mistletoe is concerned, there was a time in bygone days when it symbolized the spirit of brotherly love and neighbourly forgiveness. If two friends were at odds, or not on speaking terms, since each felt he had been wronged by the other, one would ask the local religious leader to hang a piece of mistletoe on his front door post or gate, signifying to his neighbour that he was willing to forgive and forget if requested. The other party to the quarrel, seeing the mistletoe, and wishing to make amends as well, would make a similar request, as a result of which the two parties would meet in the street between their two houses and bestow upon each other the kiss of forgiveness. The young people, glancing through the living room windows, said to one another, "This thing has infinite possibilities," and it was their youthful scheming which brought the tiny parasite into the hallway, the living room, the dining room and finally the kitchen where they could kiss away to their heart's content unnoticed or unrebuked by their elders in the other parts of the house! The customs which the Church could not discard, it consecrated, making them symbolic of some holy message and some divine truth. So holly with its thorny leaves and blood-red berries represented the Crown of Thorns that was pressed upon the Saviour's brow on Good Friday, and, when placed beside the evergreen Christmas tree, linked the mystery of His death with the mystery of His birth. The tree itself was symbolic of the dark night on which the Lord was born, while the candles that adorned its branches were reminiscent of the stars that twinkled in a deep sea of blue that first Christmas Eve.

The date of December 25 was agreed upon in the early centuries of the Christian era because it was the time when the days once more began to conquer the nights. The longest day of the year was generally June 21, after which the nights encroached upon the days until December 21 or 22 which was known as the shortest day of the calendar year. December 25 was selected since, by that time for a certainty the days once again began to swallow up the nights, symbolic of Him who came as The Light of the World to destroy the darkness of sin and death. As John wrote in the prologue to his fourth Gospel, "The light shineth in the darkness and the darkness cannot put it out."

Of all the stories that have crept in through the centuries to enrich and embellish this holy season with their distinctive and peculiar charm, none has so captured the imagination of people the world over as the tales of St. Nicholas, the fourth century Bishop of Myra, Asia Minor, who had a habit of going about distributing gifts on Christmas Eve in memory of the gifts of the Wise Men and in the spirit which had characterized their offerings to the King of Kings. As the legend spread westward, St. Nicholas became St. Nick and soon St. Nick was known as Santa Claus or Kris Kringle, and because he performed his charitable acts of kindness and gave away his good things to girls and boys at the Christmas season, he was always pictured as a jolly old man with a long white beard, dressed in a red suit and distinguished by a red cap on his head, a combination of a saint and a clown, possessing the finer qualities of each. His saintliness was seen in his benign face, his snowy white hair and long beard, and in the spirit of giving which filled his heart, while his clownliness was evident in the gaily colored costume he wore and the jolly manner in which he performed his charitable chores.

It remained for a dignified scholarly seminary professor to versify the story of St. Nicholas and make him a permanent part of every Christmas celebration. Between the fanciful tales of the brilliant story-teller, Washington Irving, and the gifted pen of an influential cartoonist, Thomas Nast, the first of whom pictured his idea of St. Nick with words while the latter did an equally effective job of expressing his ideas with a pen and a drawing board, Professor Clement Clarke Moore (1779-1863) had about all the facts he needed; only the inspiration was lacking, and that was to come in a forceful and dramatic manner at a time and place least expected.

When Captain Thomas Moore and his wife built their home "way out in the country" from the growing port city of New York, they named their place "Chelsea" after the Chelsea Soldier's Hospital near London. Situated on what is now the area between Ninth and Tenth Avenues and Twenty-Second and Twenty-Third Streets in New York City, the Moores settled down on their plantation, and it was during their residence there that a son, Benjamin Moore, was born. When this son and heir grew to manhood, he became a Christian minister, participating in the inauguration ceremonies when George Washington became the first President of The United States, and officiating at the final rites for Alexander Hamilton after his ill-fated duel with Aaron Burr. When Rev. Benjamin Moore married Miss Charity Clarke, the daughter of Major and Mrs. Thomas Clarke, he took his bride to the family estate, Chelsea, and it was there that their only child, a son baptized Clement Clarke, was born on July 15, 1779. Entering Columbia

College at the age of fifteen, a school of higher learning which his distinguished father later served as President prior to being elevated to the episcopacy and the general superintendency of the Episcopal diocese of New York, young Clement received his degree when he graduated in 1798 at the age of nineteen. While his clergyman father wanted his son to follow in the paternal footsteps, Clement decided to be a good Christian layman instead. On November 20, 1813, he married Catherine Elizabeth Taylor, a marriage that was to be blessed with nine children, and established himself at the family estate, meantime studying architecture, music and theology and in due time receiving a Doctor's degree from his Alma Mater, preparing himself for a future professorship in a school for the training of Episcopalian clergyman.

At his father's death, the son inherited Chelsea, and it was through the resident Episcopal Bishop of New York, Rev. Dr. J. H. Hobart, that the Moores, in February 1819, donated sixty lots on the site now known as Chelsea Square, to the Episcopal Diocese of New York on condition that a theological seminary be erected on the property. Two years later the donor himself was offered the professorship of Biblical Learning and Interpretation of Scripture in the newly organized graduate school, a position he was to fill for more than a quarter of a century. In between times, he managed a successful and prosperous farm and studied for the ministry, although he never presented himself for ordination as a clergyman, but was content to be a better than average layman in the Church of his father.

The year following his acceptance of the professorship, as the old year of 1822 was about to give way to a New Year, and while the happy expectancy and excitement of Christmas filled the air, the Moores made one of their regular trips into the nearby city to stock up on those supplies which their farm did not produce and purchase those last minute necessities and luxuries for the unexpected company that inevitably showed up during the joyous holiday season. Although the ground was covered with snow the day was a clear and cold one, so the father hitched up the faithful horse to the family sleigh, complete with sleigh bells and other seasonal decorations, and made the journey to and from the growing city in record time. Only this particular afternoon as he wended his way homeward through crowded streets and open country lanes, he thought of the beauty of Christmas as it affected the enrichment of Christian family life. Naturally his thoughts turned to the gifts he and his wife planned to present to their children in the name of St. Nicholas, the patron saint of all such givers, or Santa Claus, as he was then being called, and, in his imagination, he pictured what the kindly old gentleman would look like and how he would act as he came riding through the sky on his magic sleigh drawn by eight swift and sure footed reindeer, to stop for a moment on each roof, climb down the chimney into each house, however great or small, and distribute his toys and gifts as he travelled speedily around the world every Christmas Eve. In spite of the fact that Moore had already earned several degrees and was to be awarded even more in the years ahead, he had retained his talent for making "light and frivolous verses" whenever the occasion arose or the situation demanded, and it was no accident that his fertile brain began spontaneously and almost automatically creating some verses in eleven-line syllables to match the rhythmic beat of his horse's hoofs as Old Dobbin trotted through the snowy countryside enroute to the warmth and security of a familiar stall in the stable back home in Chelsea.

The household duties that demanded his immediate attention upon arriving home crowded out the ideas that had been germinating in his mind a short while before, and it was only when a family crisis arose with shocking suddenness that he drew upon them to meet an emergency that had never arisen in his family life before. Soon after his arrival home, the Moores were called to the front door of their spacious residence at the urgent knock of a neighbour who was carrying the professor's seven-year-old son in his arms and who hastened to explain that the lad had been injured when his pony slipped on a patch of ice and fell, throwing the boy against a bank and breaking his leg. The boy's pet had been so badly hurt that he had had to be destroyed, and the heartbreak added to the leg-break aggravated the lad's condition. A doctor was summoned and soon the broken bones were set and a splint applied, but when the physician heard about the tragedy his young patient had suffered, he advised the lad's father to do something to cheer him up and give him that will to live without which the miracle of healing cannot take place in the human body.

The learned scholar and erudite professor, who had publicly deplored the fact that "more of the well-disposed among my young countrymen do not devote their leisure hours to the attainment of useful learning," heeded the healer's advice and tried to assuage his little son's pain and anguish with fanciful and colorful tales of St. Nicholas and Christmas Eve. When he noticed a spark of response and remembered the rambling thoughts and little verses that had come to him earlier in the day during his return trip from the city, he began to write a poem about Christmas in which he wove together all the charming traditions of the past with the glamor of the present and the pleasant promise of the future event toward which all children look with eager eyes every December. The more he wrote and read, the more interest the injured lad displayed, and soon all bitter memory had been replaced by happy anticipation. The father's medicine worked so effectively that his son recuperated fully and lived a long and useful life of sixty more years. The lines his father wrote down that memorable Christmas Eve in 1822 were entitled "A Visit From St. Nicholas" and contained these familiar lines:

'Twas the night before Christmas when all through the house
Not a creature was stirring, not even a mouse;
The stockings were hung by the chimney with care
In hopes that St. Nicholas soon would be there;
The children were nestled all snug in their beds,
While visions of sugar-plums danced in their heads;
And Ma in her kerchief and I in my cap
Had just settled down for a long winter's nap;
When out on the lawn there arose such a clatter,
I sprang from my bed to see what was the matter.

Away to the window I flew like a flash,
Tore open the shutters and threw up the sash.
The moon on the breast of the new-fallen snow
Gave the lustre of mid-day to objects below,
When what to my wandering eye should appear
But a miniature sleigh and eight tiny reindeer,
With a little old driver, so lively and quick,
I knew in a moment it must be St. Nick.
More rapid than eagles his coursers they came
And he whistled and shouted and called them by name:
"Now Dasher, now Dancer, now Prancer, now Vixen;
On Comet, on Cupid, on Donder and Blitzen!
To the top of the porch, to the top of the wall,
Now dash away, dash away, dash away all!"
As dry leaves before the wild hurricane fly
When they meet with an obstacle mount to the sky,
So up to the house-top the coursers they flew,
With a sleigh full of toys and St. Nicholas too.
And then in a twinkling I heard on the roof
The prancing and pawing of each tiny hoof;
As I drew in my head and was turning around
Down the chimney St. Nicholas came with a bound.
He was dressed all in fur from his head to his foot
And his clothes were all tarnished with ashes and soot;
A bundle of toys he had flung on his back
And he looked like a peddler just opening his pack.
His eyes, how they twinkled, his dimples how merry;
His cheeks were like roses, his nose like a cherry;
His droll little mouth was drawn up like a bow
And the beard of his chin was as white as the snow;
The stump of a pipe he held tight in his teeth,
And the smoke it encircled his head like a wreath;
He had a broad face and a little round belly
That shook, when he laughed, like a bowlful of jelly.
He was chubby and plump, a right jolly old elf,
And I laughed when I saw him, in spite of myself.
A wink of his eye and a twist of his head
Soon gave me to know I had nothing to dread;
He spoke not a word but went straight to his work,

And filled all the stockings; then turned with a jerk,
And laying his finger aside of his nose
And giving a nod, up the chimney he rose;
He sprang to his sleigh, to his team gave a whistle,
And away they all flew like the down of a thistle.
But I heard him exclaim, ere he drove out of sight,
"Happy Christmas to all and to all a Goodnight!"

All the other Moores thoroughly enjoyed the new poem and it was copied into the family scrapbook to become one of their cherished possessions. And there in the archives it would have remained had not the daughter of a brother pastor, Rev. David Butler, an Episcopal rector in Troy, New York, been a guest at Chelsea the very next year during the Christmas holidays of 1823. When Miss Butler found the poem she was so delighted with it that she asked her host's permission to make a copy for her own use. When her request was granted by the author, she wrote down the verses ostensibly for her personal and private use only, but as she re-read them she felt they deserved a wider audience, and, unknown to Dr. Moore, she sent her copy to the editor of the Troy, New York "Sentinel" in the columns of which newspaper they were published in the issue of December 23, 1823, under the caption "Account Of A Visit From St. Nicholas or Santa Claus" accompanied by this explanatory word, "We know not to whom we are indebted for the following description of that unwearied patron of children—that homely but delightful personification of parental kindness—Santa Claus, his costume and his equipage, as he goes about visiting the firesides of this happy land, laden with Christmas bounties; but, from whomsoever it may come, we give thanks for it."

When the author was informed of his poem's success he was both delighted and dismayed, delighted that an editor thought it worth printing but dismayed because he considered it beneath his dignity as a seminary professor and unworthy of his reputation as a classical scholar. At that time he was hard at work on what he felt was to be the crowning glory of his entire life, "A Compendius Lexicon of The

Hebrew Language: In Two Volumes" the sale and use of which he feared would be curtailed if the public knew that its author had written such a piece as "A Visit From St. Nicholas." But the response of the readers was so immediate and enthusiastic that when Dr. C. C. Moore published a volume of original poems in 1844, twenty-two years after dashing off his most popular work, he included this poem with the others, thus admitting that he was the actual author.

In 1823, the Diocesan Seminary merged with the General Theological Seminary in New York City and Clement Clarke Moore became the Professor of Oriental Literature there, a post he occupied until his resignation in 1850. As the city grew, Chelsea was absorbed, so the Moores moved to a summer house in Newport, Rhode Island, where the scholarly poet passed away on July 10, 1863, five days before his eighty-fifth birthday. His body was moved to New York City in 1890 and now rests near the remains of his parents in the cemetery adjoining Trinity Church at Broadway and 155th Street, and the graves of such notables as Robert Fulton and Alexander Hamilton.

While some writers have ascribed the authorship of this Christmas favorite to other poets in the years that have intervened since it first appeared in Moore's collected poems in 1844 (see an article in "The American Weekly," December 21, 1947, in which Major Henry Livingstone is credited with having written it near the beginning of the nineteenth century), the fact that a manuscript copy of the poem in the author's own handwriting is still in existence, and that children carrying lighted candles make a pilgrimage to his grave in Trinity Churchyard every Christmas Eve to sing carols and read his poem, confirms his claim to having made this contribution to the traditions of Advent and given such a delightful picture of Santa Claus to Christmas.

HAPPY BIRTHDAY DEAR JESUS

Early Christmas morning,
  Many years ago;
When the world was sleeping,
  Blanketed with snow;
Little ones were dreaming
  What the day would bring;
Through the silence of the dawn
  I heard an angel sing:

> Happy birthday to you, Happy birthday to you,
> Happy birthday, dear Jesus, Happy birthday to you.

Down the stairs I hastened
  And beneath the tree
I beheld a vision
  Beautiful to see;
There before a manger
  On the parlor floor,
Knelt our little darling
  As she sang her song once more:

> Happy birthday to you, Happy birthday to you,
> Happy birthday, dear Jesus, Happy birthday to you.

Through the years I've wandered
  Over land and sea;
Yet each Christmas morning
  Comes this memory;
Once again I see her,
  As in days of yore,
Kneeling by that little manger,
  Singing as before:

Happy birthday to you, Happy birthday to you,
Happy birthday, dear Jesus, Happy birthday to you.

(Words and Music Copyright 1958, E. K. E.)

I wrote this song for our three children several Christmases ago, and our daughter, Mary Helene, and I introduced it to our congregation at one Sunday evening service shortly thereafter. I played the organ and sang the stanzas while she sang each Chorus as she knelt before a little manger scene in front of the altar of the Church.

Happy birthday to you, Happy birthday to you.
Happy birthday, dear Jesus, Happy birthday to you.

(Words and Music Copyright 1956, E. K. E.)

I wrote this song for our three children several Christmases ago, and our daughter, Mary Helene, and I introduced it to our congregation at one Sunday evening service shortly thereafter. I played the organ and sang the stanzas while she sang each Chorus as she knelt before a little manger scene in front of the altar of the Church.

THE STORY OF A CHRISTMAS SONG

Up on the House Top

UP ON THE HOUSE TOP

United States Highway thirty-six out of Columbus, Ohio, the state capital, passes through the towns of Westerville and Mount Vernon before reaching Gambier, Ohio, the site of Kenyon College. While Gambier can boast that one of the graduates of the college which the Protestant Episcopal Church established there in 1824, Rutherford B. Hayes (Class of 1842) became the nineteenth President of the United States, and while nearby Mount Vernon can always "point with pride" to the fact that the famous minstrel man, Daniel Decatur Emmett, composer of "Dixie" and "Old Dan Tucker" was born there, Westerville refuses to take second place to either of her near neighbours, since it was at Otterbein College in that small Ohio town that Benjamin Russell Hanby wrote his popular pre-Civil War song, "Darling Nelly Gray," which, with Harriet Beecher Stowe's "Uncle Tom's Cabin" had about as much to do with bringing on the Civil War as did the political blunders of stubborn northern abolitionists and the secessionary threats of hot-headed southern reactionaries.

Westerville, which boasted a population of three thousand in 1940 and slightly more than four thousand a decade later was originally a very small Quaker town, whose population remained constant for several years prior to the outbreak of Civil War hostilities. Significantly it served as the national headquarters for the Anti-Saloon League when this politically influential organization was established in 1909. In the intervening decades Westerville became the seat of a new college founded by the Church of the United Brethren in Christ in 1847, and named after one of the organizers of the denomination, Philip William Otterbein. Beginning in a rather humble way with a small but interested student body, this co-educational accredited liberal arts college grew in numbers and influence, serving not only its own Church but also the people of its own and surrounding communities with great effectiveness until, when its centennial was celebrated in 1947, the student body had grown to more than six hundred while its faculty numbered nearly seventy.

When the German-born clergyman, Rev. Philip Otterbein (1726-1813) accepted an invitation extended to him by Rev. Michael Schlatter to preach in Pennsylvania shortly after the middle of the eighteenth century, he had no dreams of being instrumental in the establishment of a new Christian denomination, nor any desire to participate in an undertaking of that sort. This German Reformed pastor, at the urgent insistence of his Dutch Reformed colleague, began preaching among the German settlers who were rapidly colonizing several agricultural areas in Pennsylvania, Maryland and western Virginia. Along with a fellow-evangelist, Martin Boehm, he held very effective meetings which attracted thousands of people and resulted in hundreds of converts. As one result of his success as an itinerant evangelist, Otterbein's fellow-ministers began to criticize him, either because of jealousy at his obvious success or else because of their ignorance of the motives and purposes of his enthusiasm and zeal. Undaunted, this powerful preacher organized an independent congregation in Baltimore in 1774, continuing to conduct special series of services wherever and whenever he could. As the number of converts grew, and as the clergyman saw the need for shepherding them into Churches that would minister to their spiritual needs, Otterbein and Boehm called a conference of many of their co-workers in 1800 and organized what they decided to call The United Brethren in Christ. Seventeen years later the General Conference set about providing its members with a confession of faith and a book of discipline, published in two languages so as to minister more effectively to their German and English speaking constituents. Closely allied theologically with the Methodist Church, this new group followed Methodist structure and polity, being organized into quarterly, annual and general conferences. Thirty years after the first general conference was held, their first college was established, being named Otterbein in honor of the first leader and the co-founder of their fellowship. In spite of one defection, when an ultra-conservative group withdrew from the parent body in 1889, the Church continued to grow. The climax of its development and the promise of an even brighter future came in 1946 when the union of the Evangelical Church, founded by Rev. Jacob Albright in 1803, and the United Brethren in Christ, founded by Otterbein and Boehm in 1800, was effected, and The Evangelical United Brethren Church of more than three-quarters of a million members was created.

One of the early Bishops of the United Brethren in Christ was the Rev. William Hanby, whose literary talents had led to his early appointment as editor of the denomination's official journal, "The Religious Telescope," and to his subsequent election as the publishing agent of his Church prior to his elevation to the episcopacy. The oldest son of Bishop William Hanby and his wife, Ann Mill Hanby, was born in Rushville, Fairfield County, Ohio, on July 22, 1833, and christened Benjamin Russell. As it was almost ordained or predestined that young Benjamin attend Otterbein College when he finished his elementary and high school education, the twenty-one year old student cooperated with the inevitable and matriculated there in the fall of 1854.

Pastor Hanby had long sympathized with the plight of the down-trodden Negro slave in some of the states farther south, and when some of those who had suffered at the hands of their cruel masters sought a new life by escaping and running away to one of the nearby northern or border states, Hanby's home was one of the stops on what became known as "the underground railroad" on the danger-fraught highway to freedom. During the sensitive years of his adolescence, young Benjamin had often seen his father open the back door at night to let one of those run-aways in, and he had often watched from the dark corner of an adjacent room as the clergyman fed a black fugitive and hid him away until he could resume his journey in the safety and security of the cover of darkness. He vividly remembered one particular night when an exhausted slave stopped at the Hanby house for food and shelter. While Benjamin listened, the runaway told of the tragic experiences that had driven him to leave his master and flee to freedom. The heart-breaking tale the young slave whispered that memorable night burned so deeply into the impressionable young boy's mind that he was never able to forget it. He could recount in exact detail every dramatic incident which began when the fugitive had married another slave and set up housekeeping in a tumble-down shanty on the edge of one of the fields on the Kentucky plantation where they lived and labored. But hard times had come, and his master had been forced to sell some of his slaves, and when their owner was offered $750.00 cash for the woman alone, he and his wife had been forcibly separated and she had been dragged away into Georgia, leaving him alone and heart-broken. Night after night in his dreams Benjamin could still hear the black man as he whispered his wife's name, and said, over and over again, "Nelly Gray—Nelly Gray—I'll come and get you—Nelly Gray—and when I do, nobody will ever take you from me any more." The following night the poor man resumed his journey on a trek that was to take him from his home in Kentucky through the state of Ohio to what he hoped would be eventual freedom farther north in Canada.

It was not until his junior year at Otterbein College that Benjamin Hanby attended his first slave auction. When he accidentally stumbled upon the scene, he was hardly prepared for what he saw and heard, but the shocking sight of seeing human beings auctioned off as so much cattle and sold to the highest bidder was so startling and un-nerving that for a while the young student could not believe that it was actually taking place. When he learned that such public auctions were commonplace in other parts of the country, he refused to believe his ears. As the true significance of his experience finally dawned upon him, he understood more clearly than ever before why his father had become a sworn enemy of human slavery, and when he realized that the institution of slavery was the foundation of southern economy he shuddered, because he knew that nothing short of war would ever eliminate it from the national scene.

For the next few days that memorable year of 1856 the twenty-three year old student debated the subject pro and con with some of his classmates, trying to crystallize his own thinking and sharpening his own wits so as to be able to reply intelligently to every argument advanced in favor of the continuation of slavery. Soon he was able not only to hold his own but also to confound his critics, those who advocated slavery on the basis of Old Testament teachings as well as those who defended it on the grounds of political expediency. Late one afternoon, when the memories of the past blended with events of the present, young Hanby picked up his banjo, strummed a few chords, and began to express his feelings and convictions in a song that had as its theme the experience of the runaway slave and as its immediate inspiration the sight of the slave auction and the discussions that had ensued in more recent days. Soon he was singing the haunting strains of a new song that contained these lines:

There's a low green valley by the old Kentucky shore,
Where I've whiled many happy hours away,
A-sitting and a-singing by the little cottage door
Where lived my darling Nelly Gray.

Chorus:

O my poor Nelly Gray, They have taken you away,
And I'll never see my darling any more;
I'm sitting by the river and I'm weeping all the day
For you've gone from the old Kentucky shore.

When the moon had climbed the mountain and the stars were shining too,
Then I'd take my darling Nelly Gray,
And we'd float down the river in my little red canoe,
While my banjo sweetly I would play.

My eyes are getting blinded and I cannot see my way;
Hark! there's somebody knocking at the door;
Oh, I hear the angels calling and I see my Nelly Gray,
Farewell to the old Kentucky shore.

Chorus:

O my darling Nelly Gray, Up in heaven there, they say,
That they'll never take you from me any more;
I'm coming, coming, coming as the angels clear the way,
Farewell to the old Kentucky shore.

When he put down his banjo that evening, Benjamin may have thought that he had dashed off a song that would possibly be good enough for a college minstrel show or a male quartet special when the glee club presented its annual concert, but he certainly had no idea that it would soon sweep the country, and become so popular that some unknown composer had to actually write and publish what he called "A Confederate Version" to meet the southern demand for copies. After he wrote out the words and music of his new "hit" a few days later, his college chums urged him to send it to a music publisher. He picked a Boston publishing house at random and mailed in his manuscript, fully expecting to get it back within a week accompanied by the usual formal rejection slip. Some contemporaries said later that the Otterbein student had no idea that the Boston publishers had accepted and published his song until he saw some copies of it for sale in a Columbus, Ohio, music store the following year. Others were equally as insistent that Hanby knew the Bostonians had published it for they had been thoughtful and generous enough to send him ten free copies as full payment thereof!

Anyway, when Benjamin realized that he had forgotten all about copyrighting the song in his own name, since he had not considered it worth copyrighting in the first place, he immediately wrote to the publishers and asked for an accounting. They promptly replied to the effect that since the composer had overlooked that little technicality, they had taken care of it for him, copyrighting "Darling Nelly Gray" in their own name. And they added this post-script, " 'Nelly Gray' is sung on both sides of the Atlantic. We have made the money and you the fame. That balances the account." When the poet-composer asked a lawyer to protect his interests, the attorney hastily dispatched a letter to the publishing company suggesting a settlement out of court. When this compromise was agreed upon, the author was notified that his share amounted to $100.00 of which amount the lawyer was keeping only $50 for legal fees and services involved.

The sales of the new song, however, were phenomenal and whatever glory may accrue from arousing sentiments which culminate in inter-sectional bloodshed Hanby shares with Harriet Beecher Stowe.

Following his graduation from Otterbein in the Class of 1858, the Bishop's eldest son married Mary Kate Winter, and travelled quite extensively for a year in the interests of his Alma Mater as one of her agents. Then, wearying of his nomadic life, he accepted the principalship of an Academy at Seven-Mile, Butler County, Ohio, serving in this capacity during the 1859-1860 term. In 1861, feeling the call to the ministry, and no doubt inspired by the life and influence of his consecrated father, Benjamin Russell Hanby was ordained a clergyman in the Church of The United Brethren in Christ in Lewisburg, Ohio. By that time he had written what he considered an acceptable sequel to his earlier success, a song which he named "Little Tillie's Grave," publishing it in 1860. Written in the "tear-jerker" style of the era that saw "The Letter Edged In Black" and "The Baggage Coach Ahead" bring copious tears to countless eyes, it sold fairly well because of the composer's reputation and not because of any intrinsic merit of its own. When some critics dubbed it "a weak imitation of 'Nelly Gray,' " Hanby dashed off "Old Shady," which became a favorite of the northern soldiers during the War Between The States. As the threat of war suddenly became a frightening reality, Hanby began to write songs of a more jubilant kind, turning from the sickly sentimentality of his earlier efforts to write different kinds of ballads, expressing the laughter and gaiety of the Negro people instead of their sadness, misery and woe. In this mood he penned his last "hit," "Now Den, Now Den."

After preaching for two years, the thirty-year old minister whose lilting songs rapidly became dance-hall favorites and whose music continued to set feet to tapping and hands to rhythmic clapping wherever it was played, withdrew from the active ministry, partly because he felt that some of his theological views were "not in full sympathy with those of his Church" and, more than likely, because his whole heart had never been in the ministry in the first place. While he did withdraw from the Annual Conference of his denomination in which he held membership as an itinerant clergyman, he remained an active member on the roll of one particular Church the rest of his brief and active life, never severing his connection with The United Brethren in Christ.

In 1864, Hanby accepted a position with the John Church Music Company in Cincinnati, moving the following year to Chicago to become associated with the music publishing company of Root and Cady. George F. Root (1820-1895) had not only written some of the most popular patriotic and sentimental songs during the War of 1861-1865, but he had also contributed songs to Church Hymnals and Sunday School Songbooks of the day, in an attempt to meet the growing demand for lilting tunes and simple but stirring melodies. Root, whose songs included "Tramp, Tramp, Tramp The Boys Are Marching," "The Battle Cry of Freedom" and "Just Before The Battle Mother," as well as tunes for the sacred songs "Jewels," "The Wise May Bring Their Learning" (Ellon), "There Is A Land Of Pure Delight" (Varina) and the college favorite "There's Music In The Air," encouraged Hanby to turn his own talent to songs for children as well as sacred songs for young people and adults. Their collaboration resulted in the publication of two volumes of music during 1866-1867, under the title "Our Song Birds." For this juvenile collection, Hanby composed sixty tunes in addition to penning about thirty sets of stanzas.

The autumn issue of "Our Song Birds," A Musical Quarterly for Children and Youth, For Sabbath and Day Schools, Juvenile Singing Classes and the Social Circle," dated October 1866 and entitled "The Dove," contained two original songs by Benjamin Hanby that were later to become as popular as "Nelly Gray." The first was the only successful hymn he ever wrote, a question and answer sacred song entitled "Who Is He?" While it is not included in many official denominational Hymnals in the United States today, in the 1954 edition of The Methodist Hymn Book, the official Hymnal for use in British Methodist Churches, eight stanzas of "Who Is He?" are printed with Hanby's original tune as Hymn 151; while the Hope Publishing Company of Chicago included several of the stanzas as Hymn 42 in the 1959 edition of their collection entitled "Worship And Service Hymnal," only in this instance four lines of Hanby's were grouped together to form each stanza instead of the two-line questions that comprise each separate verse in the British publication. Both agree on the Chorus or Refrain, and, except for the substitution of a "who" for a "that" and the editing of one line to read "Comes to succor, help and save" instead of "Comes to heal and help and save," it is the same hymn. The eight stanzas that are included in each of these Hymnals are in reality twelve different two-line questions which read as follows:

Who is He, in yonder stall, At whose feet the shepherds fall?
Who is He, in yonder cot, Bending to His toilsome lot?
Who is He, in deep distress, Fasting in the wilderness?
Who is He the people bless, For His words of gentleness?
Who is He that stands and weeps, At the grave where Lazarus sleeps?
Who is He to Whom they bring All the sick and sorrowing?
Who is He, the gathering throng Greet with loud triumphant song?
Lo, at midnight, who is He, Prays in dark Gethsemane?
Who is He, in Calvary's throes, Asks for blessings on His foes?
Who is He on yonder tree Dies in grief and agony?
Who is He who from the grave Comes to heal and help and save?
Who is He who from His throne Rules through all the worlds alone?

Chorus:

'Tis the Lord, O wondrous story! 'Tis the Lord, the King of Glory!

At His feet we humbly fall; Crown Him, Crown Him Lord of All!

The other original song that became universally popular was a simple little Christmas ditty that Hanby had actually composed in New Paris, Ohio, two years earlier, in 1864, and taught from a blackboard to the children until it was first printed in this 1866 publication. Originally containing six stanzas to Hanby's lilting music, the song appeared on pages 58 and 59 of "The Dove" under the caption "Santa Claus," accompanied by a tiny picture of Santa beginning his climb down a chimney with his bag of toys for the children who lived there. The music was marked "Allegretto" by the composer, but the stanzas, somewhat altered, edited and revised in the intervening decades, still have a familiar ring, for Hanby wrote these lines to be sung to his little tune:

Upon the house, no delay, no pause, Clatter the steeds of Santa Claus;
Down through the chimney with loads of toys, Ho for the little ones, Christmas joys.

Chorus:

O! O! O! Who wouldn't go, O! O! O! Who wouldn't go,
Upon the house-top, click! click! click!
Down through the chimney with good St. Nick.

Look in the stockings of Little Will, Ha! is it not a "glorious bill?"
Hammer and gimlet and lots of tacks, Whistle and whirigig, whip that cracks.

Snow-white stocking of little Nell, Oh pretty Santa cram it well;
Leave her a dolly that laughs and cries, One that can open and shut its eyes.

Here are the stockings of Lazy Jim, What will the good Saint do for him?
Lo! he is filling them up with bran, There, he is adding a new ratan!

Pa, Ma and Uncle and Grandma too, All I declare have something new;
Even the baby enjoys his part, Shaking a rattle, now bless his heart.

Rover come here, are you all alone, Haven't they tossed you an extra bone?
Here's one to gladden your honest jaws, Now wag a "thank'ee" to Santa Claus.

By the time the Chicago firm of Hall and McCreary published the twentieth edition of the collection "The Golden Book of Favorite Songs," copyright 1923, Hanby's "Santa Claus" had become "Up On The House Top" and on page seventy-five of this publication his six stanzas have been reduced to three, and "Ladies First" has prevailed in that "Nell" gets her gifts before "Will" does, reversing Hanby's original order:

Up on the house-top reindeer pause, Out jumps good old Santa Claus;
Down through the chimney with lots of toys, All for the little ones, Christmas joys.

Chorus:

Ho, ho, ho! who wouldn't go! Ho, ho, ho! who wouldn't go!
Up on the house-top, click, click, click, Down through the chimney with good St. Nick.

First comes the stocking of little Nell; Oh, dear Santa, fill it well;
Give her a doll that laughs and cries, One that will open and shut her eyes.

Next comes the stocking of little Will; Oh, just see what a glorious fill!
Here is a hammer and lots of tacks, Also a ball and a whip that cracks.

Five short months after the October 1866 issue of "Our Song Birds" came from the press, and just when some of Hanby's better music was beginning to "catch on," while he was still an employee of the Chicago firm of Root and Cady, the young composer, whose heavy dark beard made him look many years older than he really was, died in Westerville, Ohio, in a house that is now appropriately The Hanby Historic House Museum, on March 16, 1867, just four months prior to his thirty-fourth birthday.

While his years were few, he filled them with as much creative work as he could, and the fact that nearly a century after his untimely death, people are still singing his heart-tugging sentimental song, "Darling Nelly Gray," his delightful children's Christmas favorite, "Up On The House Top," and his beautiful Christmas hymn that actually surveys the life of Christ in its entirety in twelve brief stanzas, is proof that his music, while not profound or stately or dignified, nevertheless touched the common heart of his day and has been reaching the hearts of other generations ever since.

THE SEVENTH CHRISTMAS

Joseph was back in the carpenter shop,
  Mary was scrubbing the floor;
The shepherds were tending the herd and the flock
  In sight of the inn-keeper's door.
The Magi had ridden back home in the east
  Bereft of their spices and gold;
The humble and poor, looking up in the sky,
  No heavenly wonders behold!

The glamor and glitter surrounding His birth
  Had faded away in the night;
And they questioned, as back to their labor they went,
  If the angels had spoken aright.
And they pondered as year died away into year,
  At things they had seen and had heard;
And wondered if Bethlehem's baby could be
  The King, the Messiah, the Word!